THE INVENTION OF PARADISE

A spectacle in five acts by Peter C. Bener and Daniel Schmid.

Design: Franz Kaufmann. Monologue: Martin Suter. Assistant: Dominik Keller.

English Translation: Peter Hill.

Production: Buchverlag des Schweizerischen Beobachters.

Act 1: The Evocation of Paradise.   **Act 4:** Life in Paradise.

Act 2: The Encounter of Paradise.   **Act 5:** The End of Paradise.

Act 3: The Adornment of Paradise.

Cast in order of appearance:

A child, Julie, Jean-Jacques Rousseau, Friedrich Schiller, Walter and Wilhelm Tell, Gioacchino Rossini, Arnold Melchtal, Countess Mathilde, the audience of La Scala, Milan, two ladies from St. Petersburg, Manfred, the Witch of the Torrent, an Alpine hunter, Lord Byron, Peter Tschaikovsky, somnambulists, Vincenzo Bellini, the orphan Amina, Jacques Daguerre, Albert Smith, the audience of the Egyptian Hall, conquerors of Mont Blanc, Franz Niklaus König, Percy Bysshe Shelley, Mary Shelley, Frankenstein, Germaine de Staël with entourage, Bernese wrestlers, Napoleon, Empress Marie-Louise, Count Neipperg, Georg Wilhelm Friedrich Hegel, Queen Victoria, John Brown, Johann Wolfgang Goethe, Mme. Dick, ladies from Lyon, the boatwomen of Brienz, Elisabeth Grossmann, English tourists, Count Renaisse, the orchestra of La Scala, Milan, Venetian gondoliers, sportly ladies and gentlemen, King Louis of Bavaria, Josef Kainz, alphorn players, the German Emperor and Empress, girls in traditional costume, the populace, Sarah Bernhardt, César Ritz, Auguste Escoffier, a small waiter, guests, Leo Tolstoy, a Lucerne street-singer, Heidi, Friedrich Nietzsche, Herr Durisch, Richard and Cosima Wagner, Sherlock Holmes, Professor Moriarty, Empress Elisabeth, Irma Sztaray, Luigi Luccheni, a journalist, a consumptive, Waslaw Nijinsky, Berta Felber, emigrés.

My Lords, Ladies and Gentlemen,

Please make yourselves comfortable. When the lights go down, I will reveal pictures the like of which you have never seen before. They will put your ability to marvel, to thrill and to forget yourself to the test. I shall conjure up, before your very eyes, a spectre from that far off time when people still quailed before such things as apparitions. I also have a tale to tell. Not the tale of the invention of paradise (for I am a magician and not an historian), but the tale of the invention of the invention of paradise. That all the documents are authentic is a fact I need hardly mention. They all deal with Switzerland. But, strange as it may seem, the paradise in question is not Switzerland. Switzerland is merely the backcloth. A fact that is due to the inspiration of all those who have evoked this paradise and all whose belief in it was so strong that it finally became reality.

Laying out my magician's tricks for your delectation, to show you how this paradise was conjured up, encountered, fitted out and furnished, what living in it was like and how, finally, it passed away, I must rely, like all illusionists, on the suspension of disbelief, on your trust for the duration of the experiment. Otherwise, you may be lost by the wayside and I may not get you back to terra firma and reality. Afterwards you can call me a mountebank, horsetrader and dreamer, what you will. But I bid you wait until the end. When the lights go down and the curtain rises for the first time, I pray silence and your undivided attention.

Act 1: **The Evocation of Paradise.**

"A piercing scream!"

Don't worry if it gave you the fright of your life: in the salons of the Parisian nobility 200 years ago they were just as appalled by that shriek. And by the child's hand in the water.

Then: tumult on the lakeside. A beautiful lady plunges into the icy waters. Can she rescue her child?

The child is saved. But its mother catches her death of cold beneath the sombre walls of Château Chillon. Her name is Julie and her life and death are fused in a single evocation of paradise.

Julie is the heroine of Rousseau's novel "Julie ou La Nouvelle Héloïse" which appeared in 1761. It is a resounding success – greeted with enthusiasm, ironically, in precisely those circles which are the target of its barbs: the Parisian nobility. They have become so hidebound in their conventions, life at court and in the salons has lost touch with reality to such an extent that the serenity and ingenuousness of this evocation of Nature and the Natural Way of Life has them entranced, swooning with delight. Julie becomes one of the most successful books of the 18th century. And in the effete and pampered circles of the privileged classes "back to nature" is all the rage.

Read a little way into the book and you will understand better. Just imagine you are sitting, perfumed and powdered, in a brocade chair, surrounded by people who find it the height of elegance to drop their R's and L's; and you read, with your little finger stylishly cocked, in a morocco-bound volume, the following lines about life in Clarens by Lake Geneva: "A man must be sound of soul to perceive the charms that seclusion holds... If in all the world there exists a life of contentment, then it is surely the life they lead in that place. As to the question of what exactly they do in this house that they should be so happy, I believe I answered it well when I said: They know how to live – on sait vivre: but not in the sense of the French term 'savoir vivre', i.e. that one's conduct with others is bound by a dogma of fashionable customs; I refer instead to the ability to live the life that is given to Man on this earth, to the manner born, a life that will endure beyond the human span, lived in such a way that one's dying thoughts are not of a life squandered..."

Would not the rapturous picture Rousseau paints of his paradise slake your thirst for new extravagances? "...It is as thoughone were soaring above the human sojourn, leaving all mean and worldly sentiments behind, as though the soul, on approaching the ethereal regions, were to assume something of their immutable purity. In that place, one is grave without melancholy, calm without indifference, contented that one exists and has one's thoughts; all passionate cravings are exhausted, loosing the keen edge that bites, and what remains in the innermost heart is but a slight, gentle swell of emotion; thus does this heavenly region turn the passions which so torment mankind into the very instruments of happiness... In short, the spectacle has a magical, supernatural quality that enraptures both soul and senses: 'on oublie tout, on s'oublie soi-même, on ne sait plus où l'on est' – one forgets all, one forgets oneself, one no longer knows where one is."

Rousseau contemplating the wild Beauties of Switzerland.

11

Here we see Rousseau framed in his beloved landscape at the foot of the Alps: Clarens on Lake Geneva – a landscape he made famous overnight. Did he succeed in enchanting you, did you succumb to his spell, oblivious of his presence? Probably not. You are used to stronger meat. But can you imagine the

effect he must have had on an audience that was still capable of awe and enthusiasm, of fainting from sheer excitement? I hope so, for it is the very foundation of my thesis. I cannot afford to take risks at this stage. I must insist on offering another, quite different, example of the evocation of paradise:

There are two seats left in the balcony on the right. Pray be seated and watch the following scene:
A village square where a crowd has gathered. A crossbowman has just shot an apple from a boy's

head. It's an old story, I know. But imagine that you are seeing this scene for the first time and are unfamiliar with the country in which the drama is taking place:

A paradise is either empty of people or inhabited by such that blend into the landscape along with the sunset, the rocks and the lakes. Friedrich Schiller invoked paradise through its inhabitants. "Wilhelm Tell", which appeared in 1804, left a deep impression on generations of readers and theatre-goers with its glowing image of the hero fighting for liberty in the untrammelled landscape – what more effective evocation of paradise had gone before?

The "best and bravest man in all the land" was portrayed in novels, picture books, peep shows and toy theatres with tiny figures. In drawing rooms and parlours all over Europe the paradise of free men and of freedom was being evoked: "Ah, these brave Switzers, their victories at Morgarten and Sempach can compare with the glorious deeds of the Athenians at Marathon and Salamis. Handsome, stalwart fellows all, these men of the Alps."

This son of freedom is brought to his public with particular effect by one Gioacchino Rossini, hailed as the most famous composer of his day. He wrote the opera "Guglielmo Tell" which, by virtue of its attractive music and dramatic plot, achieved great popularity. He turns the already well known story into a romantic melodrama between Melchtal and an Austrian noblewoman from Gessler's entourage. All ends well thanks to Tell. Rossini, who has no more seen paradise with his own eyes than Schiller, pulls off the same trick of transporting his audience to a place "beneath the open sky, where the mind is still clear and the heart sound". He gives stage designers throughout Europe a free hand in fashioning a paradise of their own imagining.

Let me ask again if you can imagine the lasting impression this powerful evocation of paradise must have made on, say, the audience of La Scala in Milan. Can you picture it? No? Then off we go to St. Petersburg.

Въ ложѣ.

It may be less difficult for you to imagine how easily t h e s e two ladies might succumb to rapture. They are seated in the Bolshoi Theatre in Moscow or in a box at the Hermitage, the theatre of the imperial court in St. Petersburg, then the third greatest city of Europe after London and Paris. And what has enchanted them so?

It is Byron's great psychological drama "Manfred", in a free symphonic interpretation by Tschaikovsky. Thus is Manfred described: "Thy garb and gait bespeak thee of high lineage – one of the many chiefs, whose castled crags look o'er the lower valleys"; and thus: "his mien manly, and his air proud as a free-born peasant's". We encounter a Manfred beset by Faustian anguish, knowing all and yet knowing nothing, tormented by the guilt of the illicit love for his sister. And the mountain wilderness, the secret abode of fateful powers; and a hunter of chamois, embodying the ideal of the natural life and the humility of free men. Powerful emotions in a grand setting: what an exotic offering for his mundane audience!

Consider this picture for a moment. "The Mountain of the Jungfrau. Manfred alone upon the Cliffs" "...a height which none even of our mountaineers, save our best hunters, may attain." Manfred is restrained from leaping to his death by a hunter. And what words spring to his lips, what feelings! "– My mother Earth, and thou fresh breaking Day, and you, ye Mountains, why are ye beautiful? I cannot love ye." Or: "The natural music of the mountain reed – for here the patriarchal days are not a pastoral fable – pipes in the liberal air, mix'd with the sweet bells of the sauntering herd: my soul would drink those echoes."

And the words intended to be his last communion with nature:

"Ye toppling crags of ice!
Ye avalanches, whom a breath draws down
in mountainous o'erwhelming, come and
crush me!
I hear ye momently above, beneath,
Crash with a frequent conflict; but ye pass,
And only fall on things which still would live;
On the young flourishing forest, or the hut
And hamlet of the harmless villager."
"Farewell, ye opening heavens!
Look not upon me thus reproachfully –
You were not meant for me – Earth! take these
atoms!"

Some of you are doubtless eager to press on, but I would not withhold from my good listeners the sight of Manfred standing before a majestic waterfall in a deep Alpine valley: "And roll the sheeted silver's waving column o'er the crag' headlong perpendicular, and fling its lines of foaming light along, and to and fro, like the pale courser's tail, the Giant steed, to be bestrode by Death, as told in the Apocalypse.

No eyes but mine now drink this sight of loveliness." From this roaring torrent he summons up the Witch of the Alps, a graceful figure, moving wraithlike beneath the rainbow's arch to the cascading music of harp and flute. A haunting picture, is it not? Let yourselves be drawn into its eerie mood for the scene that is about to unfold.

What we shall witness next is reminiscent more of exorcism than an evocation of paradise. In fact, both are involved. Here, we see society ladies in a state of somnambulistic ecstasy. I invent nothing, nor shall I baulk at establishing a connection between this phenomenon and the evocation of paradise which is our theme.

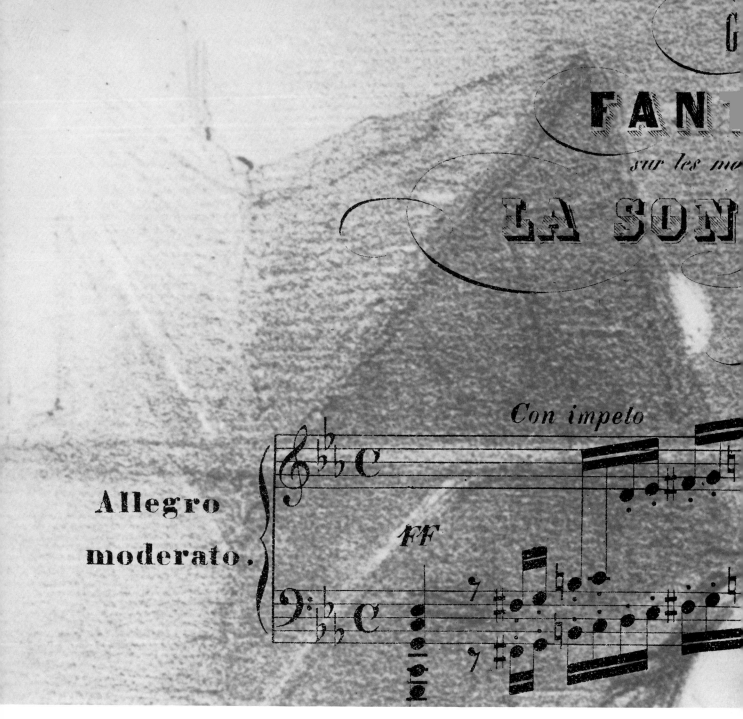

1831 saw the première of Bellini's opera "La Sonnambula", a melodrama which took the world by storm. The story tells of a beautiful orphan child, Amina, whose forthcoming marriage to a rich landowner is jeopardized by suspicions of infidelity occasioned by her habit of sleep-walking. However, Amina's second uncanny appearance as a sleep-walker convinces the villagers of her innocence.

The setting for the story is Switzerland; otherwise I would not have mentioned it. Snow-capped mountains, a mill, a shepherd's pipe, traditional costumes, peasant choirs, folk-dance melodies – all in perfect tune with the fashion of the day. Add a dash of the supernatural and the music of maestro Bellini, and it cannot fail to be a resounding success. Songs and dances based on the favourite arias from "La Sonnambula" soon begin to appear. And "somnambulism" becomes the craze in every European capital.

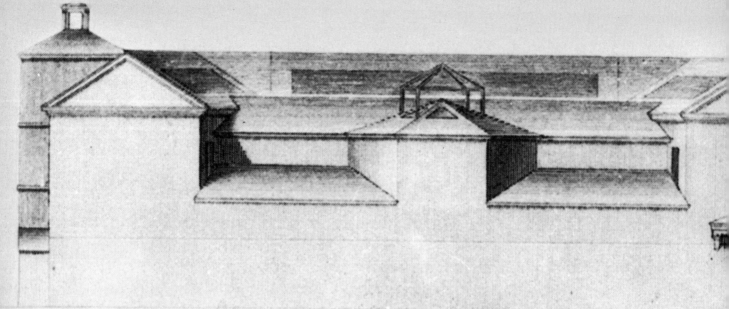

Elévation du Diorama.

Coupe du Diorama

A. Pivot de la Salle
B. Engrenage donnant le
   mouvement de rotation
C. Plan incliné portant les Galets

Terrasse régnant sur le Café
Portique extérieur
Gallerie

PLAN

And now the evocation takes on a technical note. I would like to present to you a mass medium that caused a furore in the eighteen twenties: the diorama. The inventor was Jacques Daguerre, who made his name first as a stage designer, then as originator of the daguerrotype. The diorama was, in fact, an

Coupe du Diorama sur la li...

sur la ligne C.A

D.E. *Tableaux*
F. *Galleries de ...*
G. *Emplacement d...*
      de la lumière

enormous peep-show. Citizens of Paris able to afford the entrance fee were treated to huge painted transparencies, illuminated by a system of lighting so skilful that the depth and life-like quality it gave the paintings disguised their real nature.

You are sitting in a darkened room and your eyes have gradually become accustomed to the gloom. The curtain goes up to reveal the valley of Sarnen, close enough, or so it seems, to touch. In the "faux terrain", the darkened space between audience and screen, you can make out a real Swiss chalet, a goat scurrying to and fro and three-dimensional shapes which merge perfectly into the picture. The spectacle begins: dawn comes up, then morning, noon, late afternoon and evening. In 15 minutes a whole

day unfolds before your eyes. There is a yodelling choir and the music of alphorns. The illusion is perfect. The curtain falls again, and the countless backstage helpers who have operated shutters, shades and filters, reflecting and projecting light and shade, turn the revolving platform upon which the banks of seats are mounted. You find yourself before another curtain. It rises in its turn and you are in a different country, far away, and yet close at hand.

And now I have the great honour to present my inimitable mentor, that great showmaster, narrator and popular entertainer: Mr Albert Smith! He it is who has brought paradise so close to home for hundreds of thousands, they are convinced that they have been there themselves. Let me introduce you to him:

In London in the middle of the last century, theatrical establishments bearing such names as Theatre of Mystery, Theatre of Varieties, Palace, Pavilion, Panopticon or Playhouse were shooting up like mushrooms. They held the promise of exotic dream worlds, a taste of forbidden fruit. At one of these establishments, the Egyptian Hall, Albert Smith, a globe-trotter just back from climbing Mont Blanc, is the master of ceremonies at a most unusual show based on the expedition. The hall itself is enough to cast a spell on the audience: a Swiss chalet adorns the proscenium arch; between the apron of the stage and the audience, live fish swim in a tiny lake among rushes and water lilies, their leaves sparkling in the water and gaslight to great effect. Granite blocks strewn with Alpine flowers are placed around the lakeshore. The auditorium is bedecked with the flags of the Swiss cantons and pictures illustrating each stage of the journey. Lampshades of flowers and leaves cast a pleasant, soft light. The performance can begin. Albert Smith climbs to the rostrum beside the stage: "In the name of Her Majesty, the Queen of the Alps, I bid you most humbly welcome to oysters and champagne in my Mont Blanc hall. The foremost attraction, the magnificent chalet we see before us, was built, embellished and adorned in traditional style by Herr Kehrli of Grindelwald working under my direction." Smith has specially engaged two fetching peasant girls from Gstaad. And he has brought a St. Bernard which takes round a little cart filled with Swiss chocolate during the intermission. Music and song add an acoustic element to his presentation of the Alpine world. Some of the songs are rendered by Smith himself.

In the large picture window of the chalet, a series of transparencies depicts the scenes and occurrences of the journey: the naturalistic atmosphere and tricks of lighting are inspired by the effects he has seen at Daguerre's diorama. Listen now to Smith's commentary on the ascent of Mont Blanc:

"The sun at length went down behind the Aiguille du Goûté, and then, for two hours, a scene of such wild and wondrous beauty – of such inconceivable and unearthly splendour – burst upon me, that, spell-bound, and almost trembling with the emotion its magnificence called forth – with every sense and feeling, and thought absorbed by its brilliancy, I saw far more than the realization of the most gorgeous visions that opium and hasheesh could evoke, accomplished."

44

Triomphe was commenced by Napoleon
shed until 1836. It is dedicated to the
ench army, and forms a magnificent
ce of Paris from the west. The turn-
will not bear comparison with it for an

in the *Place Vendome* is another great
and is covered with bronze reliefs cast
Austrian cannon. Our only notion of a
is a quantity of round pieces of stone
another till they reach a certain height;
lar has 2000 figures on it.—*Pay one for
he column and enjoying the view.*

es Invalides is the Chelsea Hospital of
the tomb of Napoleon, visited by our
toria in 1855. There were once 3000
church, but they were destroyed the
ies entered Paris in 1814. There are a
ry few English ones, though, if any.—

Opera must come amongst the arrange-
in Paris. The price of admission to
nd-sixpence, and for this you hear the
finest works. In London it is more
n: but the people in France go to the
dmire the performance, and in London
t fashionable to be there.—*You must
for the little footstool that is brought
r.*

t the terminus of the railway that runs
is to Marseilles, by Lyons. We are not
though. We shall stop at Dijon, eight
Paris. Dijon is an old city, all amongst
gundy, and was once the capital of the
good wine may be bought here for a
ou would pay as many shillings for at
y three at the Station for your fare.*

railway at Dijon, and then cross the
Diligence, which is like a post-chaise,
slice of an omnibus, and an old cab-
ogether. It is drawn by four or six
en people, and travels about six miles
o the *Conducteur of the Diligence.*

f the Jura we come to a *Custom-house*,
n forms the boundary between France
l here our luggage is examined. The
re severe returning into France. *Les
of the village where we are now sup-
sad, dreary place, nearly on the top of
he Custom-House Officer with one.*

p all night, nothing is so refreshing as
ieve your smarting eyes, and irritable
. Cold water closes up the pores of
olks who make a great splash and mess,
ver in a tub, are not always the cleanest.
owever, delightfully invigorating; but,
ss, water should be of the same tem-
y.—*You will gratefully pay two for a*

very handsome city, beautifully situated
e. A great many English families reside
d, since they find they can educate their
, on a small income, than in England,
ney must be spent to "keep up appear-
d. Beautiful little watches, and elegant
are made at Geneva.—*Receive six from
n excursions about the Lake; also two
n present.*

te is entirely a foreign manner of dining.
and hour, and the guests all sit down

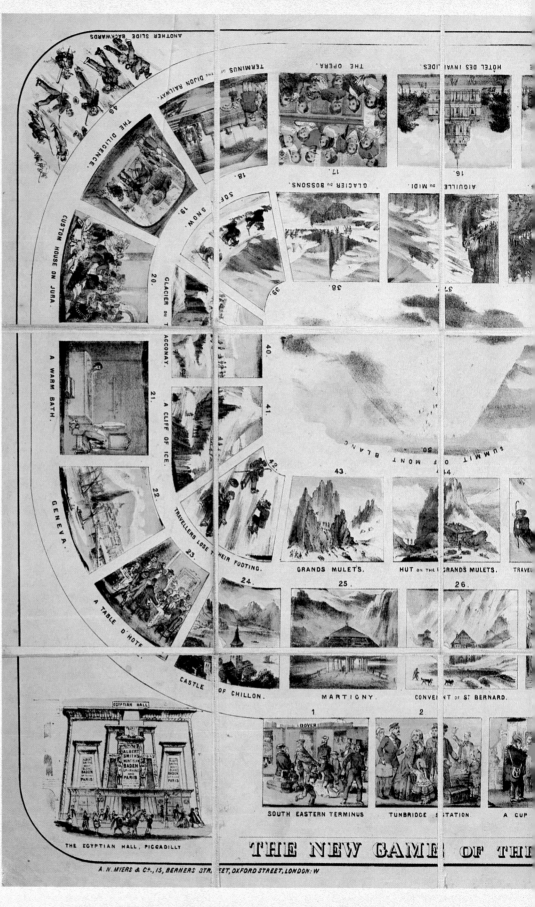

THE NEW GAME OF THE

A. N. MYERS & C°., 15, BERNERS STREET, OXFORD STREET, LONDON: W

RULES FOR PLAYING
THE NEW GAME OF THE ASCENT OF MONT BLANC.

The game may be played by any number of players. A tee-to-tum, numbered from 1 to 6 is required. A pool must be placed in the centre of the table. Each player must have 3 dozen counters.

Rule I

Each player must be provided with some kind of mark, to show his or her position on the route.

Rule II

Each player must place his or her mark on the Egyptian Hall, which is in the left-hand corner of the Game.

Rule III

To commence the game, one of the players spins the tee-to-tum. If he throws 1, he place his mark on the South-Eastern Station; if 2 on Tunbridge; if 3, he cannot move (or, if 6, he cannot move, and this rule holds good all through the game whenever he plays 3 or 6); if he plays 4 he goes to Dover; if 5, to 4 with a * in the corner of the game, and the same rule must be observed at the other corners, 24* and 46*.

Rule IV

When all playing have spun once, the first player begins again: if he spins 2 and had 2 before, he moves to 4; if he spins 1, and had 4 before he goes to 4*, and not 5, because 4* comes between 4 and 5; if he spins a 3 or 6 he cannot move, and the next player goes on.

Each player follows in turn, and whoever arrives first at the summit of Mont Blanc wins the game and takes the pool.

Rule V

At the conclusion of the game, each player is paid for the counters he still has.

The counters may be bought at twopence a dozen at the commencement of the Game.

---

1. *The South-Eastern Terminus* is the key of the continent, and the luggage wheeled along the platform may be going to any part of Europe, Asia, or Africa. With the exception of the Channel, the rails that commence at London Bridge continue to the shores of the Baltic, the Mediterranean, the Bay of Biscay, and the Gulf of Venice.—*You must pay two for your fare to Folkstone.*

2. *Tunbridge Station.* Tunbridge is a market town in Kent, about half way between London and Folkstone. Near it is Tunbridge Wells, where people go to drink the waters; and those who are quite well and have nothing in the world to do, derive great benefit from them.

3. A cup of coffee is a popular refreshment for nice ladies, and good boys and girls, as it cheers without intoxicating, and nothing is so shocking as intoxication. At the same time warm brandy and water on a winter's night, and cool pale ale on a summer's day, must not be despised.—*Pay one for a cup of coffee.*

4. Folkstone was such a dull old place twelve or fourteen years ago, that grass grew between the paving-stones, and when a stranger arrived, people ran out to look at him, and ask the news. Now it is a very flourishing place, and crowds of people daily pour through it, to and from the continent, like bees at the door of a hive.—*Pay two for your passage.*

4.* *Dover* cannot bear Folkstone, for the reason just stated, and will like it much less if ever the mails go by Boulogne. There is a great gun, on the heights, which is said to bear this inscription—

> Load me well, and sponge me clean,
> I'll carry a ball to Calais Green.

This is all nonsense.—*You must now be fined six, because, if you had not slept on the train you would have been at Dover, and you must go back to No. 2.*

5. Crossing the Channel from Folkstone to Boulogne occupies two hours and a quarter, during which time passengers scarcely know whether they are inside out, or upon their heads or their tails. Sea-sickness is a terrible malady, and often makes the dearest friends rude and inattentive to each other.—*If you do not feel the least sick here, you may take six from the pool as a reward.*

6. When you land at Boulogne, you will first be astonished at hearing such small children speak such good French. Boulogne is a very nice place, and much more entertaining and moderate than English watering-places, which are usually dull and expensive. People yawn more at Worthing in an hour, than they do at Boulogne in a month.—*On landing at Boulogne pay one for having your baggage examined.*

7. *The Grand Rue*, or High Street of Boulogne is very lively on market day; and the clean white caps of the female peasants are much prettier than the fusty old bonnets of the Covent Garden basket-women. When you go to market in France, never give what they ask for anything, by which simple plan you will get things cheaper.—*Spend two for the good of the market.*

8. *Boulogne Station* is just out of the town, and is very comfortable compared to the old Diligence office. Before the railway opened, it took twenty-four hours to get to Paris, but now the train does it in six. The old road was very ugly; the beginning was like the end, and both resembled the middle.—*Pay six for your fare.*

9. At *Amiens* the train stops twenty minutes for refreshments; and a cutlet, or half a small fowl, with nice hot gravy and a little decanter of claret, is by no means a bad amusement. Here the railway divides, and one branch goes up to Belgium and the north—the other to Paris.—*Pay one for some refreshment.*

10. *The Paris Station* is some little distance from the centre of the city. During the omnibus ride the traveller will notice the height of the houses and numbers of sign-boards; the bars in front of the butchers' and bakers' shops; the noise the drivers make at the horses; the absence of bonnets among the women; and the gaudy advertisements upon the blank walls.—*Present each lady present with three counters.*

11. *The Palais Royal* is a quadrangle of elegant shops and eating-houses surrounding a beautiful garden. It is quite a city in itself, and a person might live here for ever, and find everything he wanted, without leaving it. It is the paradise of children in fine weather, and of idlers when it rains, for all the shops are under arcades, like those in the Covent Garden Piazza.—*Pay three for your dinner in the Palais Royal.*

12. The Bourse, which means "Purse," is the Exchange of Paris; and fortunes are made here, out of nothing, as incomprehensibly as in London. We have no building in town so handsome as the Bourse—in fact, we don't shine at all in architecture, and so had better say nothing about it.—*If you are fortunate enough to get to the Bourse, receive twelve from the pool for your expenses in Paris, and one from each of the players.*

13. *Notre Dame* is the cathedral of Paris, and is a large gloomy building not very remarkable for beauty of decoration compared with other continental churches. Nobody knows much about its original construction, but it is said a great portion has been built eight or nine hundred years.—*Pay one for ascending the tower.*

14. *The Arc de* in 1809, and not [...] victories of the [...] object at the entr[...] pike at Kensingto[...] instant.

15. *The Colum[...] ornament to the ci[...] out of Russian an[...] column, in London[...] put on the top of o[...] but this beautiful p[...] going to the top o[...]

16. *The Hôtel [...] France. It contain[...] gracious Queen V[...] trophy flags in th[...] night before the A[...] great many still—v[...] Return to No. 14.*

17. *A visit to t[...] ments during a s[...] the pit is only thr[...] first artists and t[...] than double that [...] Opera because they[...] because they thin[...] not forget to pay [...] you by the box-ke[...]

18. Here we ar[...] all the way from [...] going so far as tha[...] or nine hours from[...] the vineyards of B[...] province. A bottle[...] few pence, such as[...] an English hotel.—

19. We leave t[...] Jura mountain in [...] a six-inside coach[...] riolet, all fastene[...] horses, holds seve[...] an hour.—*Give on[...]

20. On the top[...] because this moun[...] and Switzerland, [...] search is much n[...] Rousses is the nam[...] posed to be. It is [...] the pass.—Present[...]

21. Having sat [...] a *warm bath* to r[...] skin, and dusty hai[...] skin: so that those[...] and shudder and sh[...] A cold plunge is, [...] for perfect cleanlin[...] perature as the bod[...] warm bath.

22. *Geneva* is a [...] at the end of the lak[...] in the neighbourhood[...] children better her[...] where so much mo[...] ances," as it is call[...] articles of jewellery[...] the pool, to spend [...] from each gentlema[...]

23. *A Table d'h[...] It is at a fixed pric[...]

Intermission. Smith distributes leaflets certifying that he has indeed climbed the peak. During the break, a majestic panorama of the Gotthard route is unfurled before the stage. At a stand built in chalet-style dice games are on sale for those members of the audience who wish to ascend Mont Blanc in their own homes.

enerally very silent,
his neighbour, and
loud in French. So
nore substantial, and
d for a shilling in
nent.—*Pay two for*

the other end of the
red it famous by his
l crowds of tourists
a, however, abounds
Rousseau, Voltaire,
will always be con-
boat.

aid to be below the
. The Prior Bonne-
and you see the ring
and the stone floor
very good man—had
ave gone out with a
emonth.—*Give three
n.*

lace. It is also very
; so people arrive at
oon as they can. Its
f foolish; and in the
fevers by the mos-
severe.

lmost in the clouds—
dozen monks always
itable and pious acts.
gny, and the road is
four miles. By this
Alps in 1800, before
esent the monks with

the St. Bernard, is
or people who have
and the temperature
, like mummies, for
fatal accidents since
s on the road.—*Pay
e lost relations and
25.*

s, of whom are told
gh—are said to be a
he Pyrenean mastiff.
here were only three
of these, *Diane*, to
our of presenting it
and good-tempered,
the paths under the
the dogs.

tiful pass, and leads
ccession of precipices,
nearly all the way,
re is a good inn here,
untain mutton chops,
f a bad thing for a

w of the *Valley of
ises.* Chamouni itself
—very nearly as high
s a poor little village,
destroyed by fire in
g built, and, without
nd flourishing place.
*seen the Valley of
for the treat.*

deserve that name.
aggling lane, which

appears to be paved with stone pears, having their pointed ends uppermost. But it must be recollected that Chamouni and Mont Blanc are not in Switzerland, but in Savoy, which is a very dirty country.—*Spend two in the Swiss carved wood-work.*

32. Here is the court-yard of the *Hotel* where we are stopping, kept by M. Tairraz. Although in such a wild region, we can eat and drink and sleep as comfortably as in Paris or London. Very often, during the autumn, there are scarcely beds enough for half the visitors.—*Pay three for your room at the Hotel.*

33. *The Baths of St. Gervais* are beautifully situated in a valley and during the season are filled with visitors who prefer the quiet of the residence to the bustle of Chamouni. You must understand that people who go to baths for their health have seldom a great deal the matter with them, but they like the change, the food, the good hours, the society, and the leisure.—*Pay one to the pool.*

34. *The Source of the Arveiron.* The Arveiron is a river formed by the melting of the ice on the Mer de Glace, or, as it is sometimes called, thé Glacier du Bois. It sometimes flows from a vast icy arch as here represented. Sometimes, as is the case at present, this arch gets stopped up, and then it bursts from the side of the glacier in a cascade. —*You must return to No. 29, and pay two to each lady present.*

35. *The Mer de Glace,* or "Sea of Ice," is a large glacier, so called because its huge ridges are fancied to bear some resemblance to the waves of a sea frozen during a storm. Visitors in Chamouni can go completely across it, but this requires guides, as its chasms are very deep and dangerous. —*Pay one to the pool for a walking pole.*

36. *The Pelerins* was the first house-of-call on the way up Mont Blanc, and was celebrated for a beautiful cascade. The water, from a great height, fell upon a stone, which threw it up into an enormous curve; but in 1852 a torrent carried the stone away, and spoiled the waterfall.—*Spend two here for the benefit of the house.*

37. *The Aiguille du Midi* is one of those gigantic peaks of granite which rise like sentinels round Mont Blanc from the valley of Chamouni. The path to the glacier winds round its side. It is a mere ledge, in some places scarcely more than a foot broad, with a rock on one side and a precipice on the other.

38. *The Glacier du Bossons* is one of the most beautiful valleys of ice that descend from Mont Blanc to Chamouni. Sometimes it is very easy to cross, but now and then vast crevices open; and then it is dangerous, and requires great caution.—*As this is the first time you have been on the glacier, you may receive two from each player, and six from the pool.*

39. Here our party gets on some soft snow. The guides dread this more than anything. Not only is the labour of marching considerably increased, but the snow sometimes masks the crevices with a false appearance of solidity.— *Pay one as you get out of this soft snow.*

40. *The Glacier du Tacconay* is always full of large crevices. Here you see an accident by which a guide, named Tissay, was nearly lost. He slipped on the ice, and went over the precipice. If the party had not been fortunately tied together with cords, he would have been dashed to pieces.—*Pay two here to have a new rope, in case you should slip.*

41. This is another difficulty on the same glacier, and shows the manner of scaling a cliff of ice. A guide climbs up first, by cutting some notches for his hands and feet with a hatchet. Then he helps the others up with a cord, and the luggage is made into bundles, and also pulled up.—*Pay two for the benefit of the guide who goes up first.*

42. Very often the travellers lose their footing, and slide down huge declivities of the ice on the glaciers. If there is

a crevice below, this is dangerous; but if the slide merely ends in soft snow, it makes good fun.

43. *The Grands Mulets* are rocks that rise through the snow at a height of 10,000 feet above the level of the sea. The party always fixes its bivouac here, for it is safe from avalanches. The rocks are reached about four o'clock in the afternoon; and when the people at Chamouni find out, with telescopes, that the travellers have arrived so far, they fire guns.—*As you have reached the Grands Mulets, you are entitled to receive six from the pool, and one from each player.*

44. *The Hut on the Grands Mulets* was built in 1852. Before this, travellers had no shelter beyond rugs and wrappers and, sometimes, when bad weather came on, suffered very severely. Since the hut has been built, an excursion to the Grands Mulets is quite a common thing, and several ladies have reached the rocks. There is not a great deal of room, though, inside the hut; and the guides are so afraid of cold and fresh air, that they shut up all the windows, and then begin to smoke. Although very tired, the travellers seldom sleep much—anxiety for their success in the ascent, and the novelty of the situation, tend to keep them wide awake.—*Pay three to keep the hut in good condition for other travellers.*

45. You must be more careful, or you will not reach the summit; if it had not been for your pole, you would have gone down a crevice and never been heard of again. —*Pay two to make you a little more steady, and go back to No. 37.*

46. *The Grand Plateau,* although nearly level, is the most treacherous part of the journey, as it is exposed to all the avalanches which descend from Mont Blanc. It was here that three guides were carried away by a snow-slip in 1820, when Dr. Hamel tried the ascent, and they were never heard of again.—*Give three for the benefit of the families of those guides who perished here.*

46.* Another slide backwards: we must be more careful now.—*As you have been careless, you must pay two to the pool.*

47. The rarefaction of the air has a very painful effect upon some persons. They have great difficulty in breathing and are seized with nausea, and sometimes bleeding at the nose. The poor fellow cannot get on any further. He must give up the attempt and get back to the Grands Mulets as well as he can.—*Pay two for the benefit of the sick man who is compelled to return, and go yourself to 42.*

48. *The Mur de la Côte* is perhaps the most dangerous part of the ascent. It is an iceberg, almost upright, and the steps are cut with a hatchet. Should the foot slip, or the baton give way here, it would lead to instant destruction: and so, very great firmness and caution are necessary.— *Receive two from each player for having surmounted this dangerous part of the ascent.*

49. The travellers slip and stagger about a great deal on the last ascent—the actual dome of Mont Blanc; and sometimes are quite bewildered, and require to be almost dragged up by the guides.—*You must pay for your carelessness, and this time, as you are so near the summit, you must pay six, and you must return to No. 42.*

50. Here we are, on the *Top of Mont Blanc*—15,665 feet above the level of the sea! It is half-past nine in the morning, and we have been over six-and-twenty hours from Chamouni. When we get back to the village, we shall be received with guns, flowers, and a band of music. And so all our peril is over, and we will open a bottle of Champagne, and cry

"GOD SAVE THE QUEEN"

—*For having been the first of your party to reach the top, you will receive all the counters that are in the pool, and with these the congratulations of your fellow-tourists.*

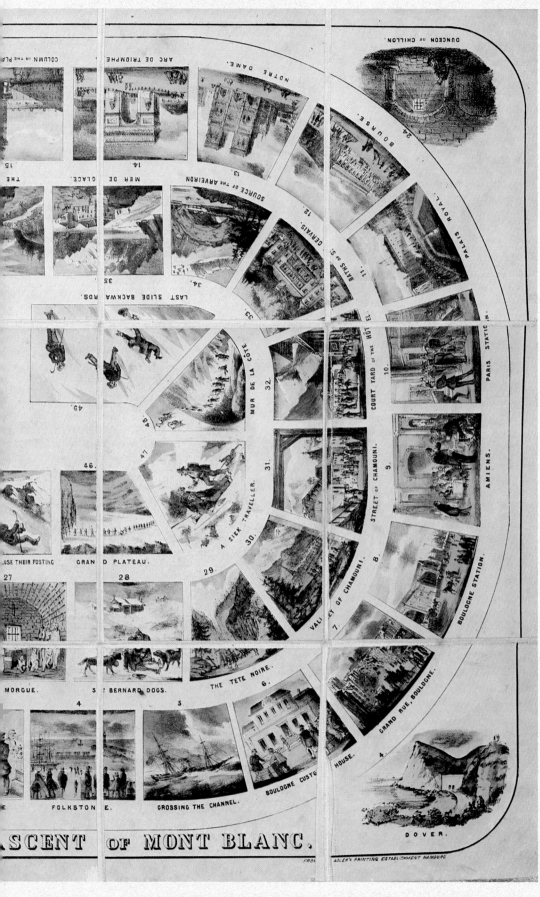

ASCENT OF MONT BLANC.

together at a large table. They are
everybody being too proud to talk t
usually afraid to ask for anything ou
the dinner is very solemn. A cleaner,
more wholesome meal can be procu
London than anywhere on the Con
your dinner.

24. *The Castle of Chillon* is quite a
Lake of Geneva. Lord Byron has rend
poem, "The Prisoner of Chillon;" ar
visit it every year. The Lake of Gene
with associations; and the names of
Madame de Stael, Byron, and Gibbon
nected with it.—*Pay one for the steam*

24.* *The Dungeon of Chillon* is
level of the lake, but this is a mistak
vard was confined there for six years,
in the pillar to which he was chaine
worn by his constant walk. He was a
he been a criminal, perhaps he would
ticket of leave at the end of a twelv
because you are free, and not in pris

25. Martigny is a wretchedly dull
unhealthy, and surrounded by swamps
night, and get off in the morning as
population is stunted, diseased, and ha
summer, travellers are tormented inte
quitoes, whose poisoned bites are ver

26. *The Convent of St. Bernard* is
8200 feet above the level of the sea!
live here, and devote their lives to cha
It takes a day to reach it from Mart
unfit for wheels for the last three or
pass Napoleon took his army over the
beating the Austrians at Marengo.—*P*
six, for their hospitality.

27. *The Morgue,* or deadhouse, o
a solemn sight. The bodies of the p
perished in the snow are kept here,
is so low that they remain preserve
years. There have, fortunately, been n
1850, in consequence of improvemen
one for those poor creatures who h
friends in the snow, and return to N

28. The renowned *St. Bernard D*
such wonderful stories—not true, tho
cross between the Newfoundland and
The breed is becoming rare. In 1853,
at the convent. The monks gave on
Mr. Albert Smith, and he had the h
to Her Majesty. They are powerfu
and their great use is to scent out
snow.—*Pay two towards the keep of*

29. *The Tête Noire* is a very bea
from Martigny to Chamouni. It is a s
waterfalls, rocks, forests, and torre
and can be walked in seven hours. T
about half-way, and a couple of mo
with a glass of good wine, is not h
pedestrian.

30. Here we have our first vie
Chamouni, from which Mont Blanc
is 3370 feet above the level of the se
as the top of Snowdon, in Wales. It
and what there was of it was nearly
1855; but now splendid hotels are be
doubt, some day it will be a large
—*As this is the first time you ha*
Chamouni you must pay six to the p

31. The streets of *Chamouni* sca
The main thoroughfare is a long

And the show continues: "Before we could tackle the summit, which was beckoning to us in the back-ground, we had to climb the terrible Mur de la Côte. ...There is nothing below but a chasm in the ice more frightful than anything yet passed. Should the foot slip or the baton give way, there is no chance for life – you would glide like lightning from one frozen crag to another, and finally be dashed to pieces, hundreds and hundreds of feet below in the horrible depths of the glacier... With muscular powers already taxed far

beyond their strength, and nerves shaken by constantly increasing excitement and want of rest – with bloodshot eyes, and raging thirst, and a pulse leaping rather than beating – with all this it may be imagined that the frightful Mur de la Côte calls for more than ordinary determination to mount it... We reached the foot of the last ascent, the Calotte, as it is called – the 'cap' of Mont Blanc... I was scrambling almost on hands and knees, and then... I looked round, and saw there was nothing higher. I was on top of Mont Blanc."

Albert Smith (and who is better qualified than the master conjuror of our paradise?) speaks thus of the view from Mont Blanc: "As a splendid panorama, the sight from the Rigi Kulm is more attractive".

I have been saving up something special to conclude my story about the evocation of paradise: the predecessors of Daguerre and Smith.

Painted with translucent watercolours, pressed between two sheets of glass and lit from behind with flickering lamps, these pictures of Swiss landscapes even moved the aging Goethe to attest publicly to

their value as art. We are speaking of the famous "Diaphanorama" with which the painter Franz Niklaus König toured Germany in 1820. That you see them here is due in part to the exceptional quality of the original material. And to the fact that they are so powerful an evocation of paradise, you are finally convinced that you have encountered its true heart.

Let us accompany Herr König for a moment on his tour of the "most remarkable sights of Switzerland". He leads us into the wilds of nature, to the chamois hunt on the upper Grindelwald glacier, and to more peaceful scenes, such as the tranquil evening meal of a peasant family.

In the Bernese painter's own words:

"...the Tell chapel on the shores of the Lake of Lucerne by night! Consider, ladies and gentlemen, how the bright moon rises from out of the dark clouds and is reflected in the rippling water. Join the guests

who have just alighted on the bank, the way to the chapel lit by a flaring torch held aloft by one of their company."

Act 2: **The Encounter with Paradise.**

Now the evocation is complete. The ideal country of tranquil lakes, towering peaks, wild ravines and gentle pastures, inhabited by a proud, free nation – with a different brand of nobility to that of the metropolitan aristocracy – is firmly planted in the minds of an enraptured public. Very few of the initiates have actually set foot in their paradise. But its evocation has made so profound an impression that a personal encounter with the real thing is unlikely to shake the image conjured up by books and theatrical spectacles. Would you like to witness the first attempts of the elect to measure their imaginings against the reality? Do you want to see what happens when the upper classes of the period, given to histrionics as they most surely are, begin to act out their notions of paradise in its true setting?

Up and away! The promised land calls.

Do you remember? We stood on this very spot on the shore of Lake Geneva in the first act. A shrill scream, a tiny hand in the icy waters, Julie plunging into the waves, the appalling mishap which results in her death. It was Rousseau who took us to Château Chillon. You will recall the stir caused by his story and the landscape in which it unfolds. You will not be surprised, then, to find the following company when you arrive:

The year is 1816. Byron, at 28 the brightest star in the English literary firmament, has fled to Switzerland leaving a trail of scandal behind him.

He is staying in a rented villa at Cologny with Shelley, aged 24, who is yet to achieve stardom, and Mary Godwin, 19, later to be Mrs. Shelley.

The young companions go out riding by moonlight and boating on the lake. One such boating party inspires Byron to write a "Sonnet to Lake Leman". What wonderful confirmation of my thesis that our paradise was born and nurtured in the hearts and minds of a few great men and women. Allow me to quote his words:

"Rousseau – Voltaire – our Gibbon – and De Staël – Leman! these names are worthy of thy shore,

Thy shore of names like these! wert thou no more, / Their memory thy remembrance would recall:

To them thy banks were lovely as to all, / But they have made them lovelier, for the lore

Of mighty minds doth hallow in the core / Of human hearts the ruin of a wall

Where dwelt the wise and wondrous; but by thee, / How much more, Lake of Beauty! do we feel,

In sweetly gliding o'er thy crystal sea, / The wild glow of that not ungentle zeal,

Which of the heirs of immortality / Is proud, and makes the breath of glory real!"

Byron's encounter with paradise moves him to write "Manfred", that soulful drama which sent the two Russian ladies into raptures in the first act. We owe the next scene and Byron's sombre tale "The Prisoner of Chillon" to a visit he made to the eponymous château:

Chillon et la Dent du Mid...

"There are seven pillars of Gothic mold, in Chillon's dungeon deep and old;

There are seven columns, massy and grey, dim with a dull imprison'd ray,

A sunbeam which hath lost its way,

And through the crevice and the cleft of the thick wall is fallen and left:

Creeping o'er the floor so damp, like a marsh's meteor lamp:

And in each pillar there is a ring, and in each ring there is a chain;

That iron is a cankering thing..."

It is evening in Cologny near Geneva. A piercing wind is whipping the rain against the windows of the Villa Diodati. A light burns in the drawing room. A young lady and two young men are huddled by the fire, reading ghost stories. They work themselves into a mood of unnatural excitement. One of them becomes so frenzied he imagines he can see eyes peering out from the girl's bosom. His reason becomes so unhinged that smelling salts are needed to bring him round. In this exalted mood the friends decide to write their own horror stories that very night. The young lady retires. Byron and Shelley sit for a time by

the fireside, sipping wine, and jot down fragmentary thoughts. In the young lady's room on the first floor a light is burning. It remains lit throughout the long hours of darkness. The wind rattles the willow branches against the bull's-eye window panes. Mary Godwin sits by the flickering candle-light and drafts out the story of a doctor who is obsessed by the idea of creating a human being from the parts of corpses. His name is Dr. Frankenstein, and Mary Shelley, as she will later be known, owes her place in posterity to the chilling tale dreamed up on that evening in paradise.

This rugged, down-to-earth aspect of paradise is witnessed and recorded by one of the most influential women of the period around 1800: Madame de Staël. She lives in exile in her château at Coppet on the shores of Lake Geneva. As a matter of fact, she is one of the reasons why Byron is so attracted by the area.

In her book "De l'Allemagne", which to this day affects the way the French see their Germanic neighbours, Madame de Staël describes a country fair or "Älplerfest" in Interlaken. The festive procession makes a deep impression on her: "In the middle of the festivities my eyes filled with tears. The feeling was reminiscent of those happy, melancholic days when one rejoiced at the return to health of a loved one." The wrestling matches in the Bernese manner prompted her to remark that the "Schwinger", as the

protagonists are called, possessed considerable strength and skill, but that these qualities would be of no military value in the face of modern artillery tactics. However, she concludes her report with the following words: "May this same festival be held year in year out at the foot of these same mountains! The outsider stands before them as though beholding a miracle, the Swiss love them dearly; they are alike to a refuge in which the magistrates and fathers have joint care of the common folk and their children."

Madame never travelled alone. Her folkloristic trip to Interlaken was no exception. We owe this intelligence to her description of the manner in which tourists comported themselves in the Switzerland of that day: "A sight to be savoured: young Parisians walking in the narrow streets of Unterseen, suddenly finding themselves set down in the valleys of Switzerland. They heard naught but the roar of waterfalls, saw only mountains, and asked themselves whether this solitude would bore them enough to return to the world with their taste for its pleasures refreshed."

You are probably wondering why Madame de Staël lived in exile: she was banished by no less a person than Napoleon, the glorious conqueror of our wintry paradise, who was himself to suffer the fate of banishment only fourteen years after his triumphant crossing of the Great St. Bernard. His second wife, Marie-Louise, the daughter of the Austrian Kaiser Franz, did not follow him into exile. She sided instead

with her father, becoming thereby an enemy of France. On the advice of his cunning chancellor Metternich, the Kaiser sent his daughter on her travels to try and turn her thoughts to other things. Count Neipperg, a notorious lady-killer with the nickname "der schöne Gehenkte" (literally "the handsome hanged man"), was assigned as her travelling companion.

Needless to say, their tour includes a sojourn in paradise. And it is on the Rigi that the inevitable finally occurs. On the night of September 24th, bad weather forces the illustrious party to spend the night in a simple pension at the summit. Normally, with hotel rooms arranged in a suite, a servant would sleep before Marie-Louise's door. But here the rooms are separate and open onto a corridor. Neipperg steals unnoticed into the lady's bedroom. Were it not for a love-letter to Neipperg that Marie-Louise carelessly leaves in a map of Switzerland, I would never have learned of this historic act of adultery.

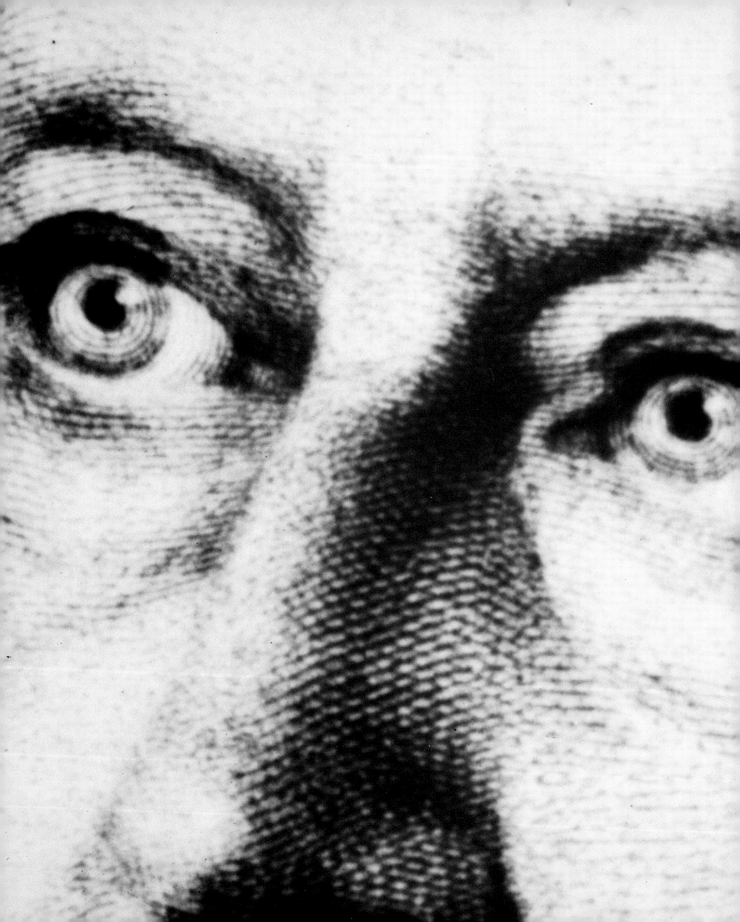

Allow me now to withdraw behind the scenes and leave the stage to a colossus of the mind who is about to encounter the colossus of stone and ice that is our Alpine paradise: Georg Friedrich Wilhelm Hegel. In the summer of 1796, aged 26, the far-sighted thinker and epoch-making philosopher, then a private tutor, spent a hiking holiday in Bernese Oberland. In writing down his observations he describes the paradise he really sees and not the one he wants to see:

"After about an hour's walk, the path begins to follow the twin streams of the Litschenen, their greyish-white turbid water, tumbling forth on a stony bed in a ceaseless tumult which often grows, where the torrent is narrowest and must force its foaming passage, to a thunderous roar such that any traveller, though he be unaccustomed to it, would weary after several hours in its company."

"In the evening we visited the Staubbach. We had already caught glimpses of it on the way, particularly from the inn, and despite its nearness it seemed no more than an inconsiderable thread of water (...) hardly a just reward for the toil and trouble of our day's exertions (...)"

"We were too tired to await the fairy dance of moonlight after nightfall. And similarly disinclined to wait for the famous rainbow to appear (...) We ate a hearty meal of eggs, ham, some roast, and excellent strawberries."

"The height of the rocky precipice from which it falls has in itself a certain grandeur, the actual cataract of Staubbach is less imposing. All the more charming, then, is the graceful, unrestrained play of water and spray. Not being in the presence of a power, a great force, the mind does not dwell on the constraints and compulsions of Nature; and that which is alive, constantly dissolving and bursting asunder, not united in one mass, inexorably moving forth in ceaseless activity, conjures up more the image of random play."

On contemplation of waves: "Their form is in constant flux, one supplants the other, to be supplanted in its turn, an unchanging picture in the eye of the beholder, yet he knows it to change momently."

"Nowhere is one's impression of Nature's inexorable quality so clear than when contemplating the eternal futility of the eternal dashing of waves against such rocks as these!"

"In the valley we found spring water which, when mixed with kirsch, proved most refreshing."

"Today, we saw this glacier only half an hour away and found it to hold little of interest to the eye. A kind of seeing it may be called, but to the mind it offers no further occupation whatsoever."

"The appearance of the lower part of the glacier (...) has neither grandeur nor charm. Further up, the ice is formed in pyramidal shapes of purer blue, contrasting with the dirty colour of the lower parts, and can,

if one so will, be called more beauteous."

"Apart from the satisfaction of seeing such a glacier from so near that I might touch it and regard its ice, I felt nothing."

"...Yet the inhabitants of these parts live in the awareness of their subjugation to the power of Nature, and are given to a stoical submissiveness when its destructive force is unleashed. If their dwelling is shattered, buried or washed away, they build another in the same place or close at hand. Though, on a particular path, men are often crushed by falling rocks, it will still be used. What a contrast to the town-dweller, who (...) would not suffer with such imperturbability the forces of nature. This latter would be needy of solace and find it in prattle, finally convincing himself that the mishap was nonetheless to his advantage. To demand of him that he forgo any recompense would be like demanding that he relinquish his God."

"The senses are in no way impressed or moved to awe and admiration by contemplating the eternal quality and supposed nobility of these mountains. The sight of these eternally dead masses provokes in me a single and, in the long run, tedious thought: It is thus –

Es ist so. »

The little woman seated here, so engrossed in a watercolour of Mount Pilatus she has painted herself, is none other than the unyielding ruler of the British Empire during a visit to paradise: Queen Victoria who gave her name to an age and its moral principles.

THE VILLA WALLIS, LUCERNE, THE TEMPORARY RESIDENCE
OF QUEEN VICTORIA IN SWITZERLAND.

SALON DE LA REINE

CHAMBRE A COUCHER DE LA REINE

The year is 1868. The Queen is staying with her daughter and her manservant, John Brown, at the Villa Wallis. She sits at the window watching the light fade over Lucerne, the lake and Pilatus. The view is a familiar one. Many years ago she was captivated by Albert Smith's diorama (you will remember), and as a young bride she sojourned in the Alps with her prince. At home, in the park of Osborne House on the Isle of Wight, her husband built a Swiss chalet for their children, who have long since reached adulthood. It is six years since the death of the Prince Consort for whom she still grieves. She is

THE QUEEN'S VIEW, LAKE OF LUCERNE, FROM THE PENSION WALLIS

approaching fifty and has a strenuous journey behind her. Instructions have been given to prepare her bed early, for tomorrow she plans to ascend the Rigi. The Queen of the Seas seeks a meeting with the Queen of the Alps.

Whether Victoria actually did climb the Rigi is a moot point. However, such is the image we have of her that we are prompted to record this grand encounter, whatever the verities of the matter:

On the day, the trip proved quite adventurous. In order to remain incognito, the Queen changes her clothes several times and switches from carriage to mount and back again, mingling with other travellers on the terraces above the lake. Towards evening she reaches the modest pension close to the summit and spends a brief night there. It is still dark the following morning when they climb the short path to the summit in the company of other bleary-eyed figures, well wrapped against the cold. John Brown carries a chair for her use on the viewing platform. She sits down to await the best-known sunrise in the world.

The observation tower is shrouded in thick mist. The morning is cold, damp and grey. Lost in thought, the tiny figure muses on the past, imagining herself on a reviewing stand as endless columns of soldiers march past. The mist begins to lift, turning a lighter grey, then white, then almost translucent.

Suddenly, the sun breaks through and a panorama opens before the Queen, making all the toil and discomfort worthwhile.

And then Victoria pays the Rigi a compliment which can only be fully appreciated if one knows how fond she is of the Scottish Highlands: "We consider the skyline of our dear Highlands distinctly flat.

"A natural scene of some grandeur, interesting in all its aspects, though within the bounds of our imagining and comprehension."

Goethe is not exactly overwhelmed by the sight of the Rhine Falls. He does spend a day finding the most impressive vantage point from which to view the spectacle, but there are bounds to his enthusiasm. However, he is always in mind of his duty to posterity: "This phenomenon of nature cannot be painted or described so often that we shall ever tire of it." – "It surges and boils and hisses and roars – the versifying is not amiss." – "On longer contemplation the movement appears to increase – and so it does." Hm.

NOTICE

MADAME DICK, resident at No. 13 in the yellow quarter, opposite the French church, has the honour to inform the public that the four young ladies of Lyon presently lodged at her establishment have contracted a venereal affection; she therefore deems it her duty to inform her esteemed clientèle that she is in no way answerable for any gentleman who has already been infected by the said ladies, or who would please still to infect himself.

On the other hand, she has the pleasure to inform her honoured friends and fellow citizens that four new damsels of the best and freshest sort are due to arrive this coming week, and that all *amateurs* and friends of this establishment are respectfully invited to taste of their charms.

Frau Dick, wohnhaft gelb Quartier Nro. 13 gegen der französischen Kirche über, thut E. E. Publikum zu wissen; daß sich leider die bey ihr

---

Berne seems to have made more impression on Goethe. "In Berne, on the 8th, I was unable to finish early with the wigmaker, and called on several people who were not at home, so I used the occasion to roam through the town. It is the most attractive of all those we have seen; the houses are all built along similar lines in whitish-grey sandstone; the uniformity and cleanness within is most pleasant to behold, especially as one feels that nothing is mere frivolous decoration or the common run of despotism. The civic buildings of Berne itself are large and sumptuous, though lacking any display of ostentation that would assail the eyes."

What bearing does the notice put up by Madame Dick, "resident at No. 13 in the yellow quarter, Berne", have on Goethe's encounter with paradise? Who knows.

The Giessbach Falls are said to be one of the most spectacular sights in paradise. And on the way

there we find another tourist attraction, if anything, better known: the lovely boatwomen of Brienz.

When you go to the quayside at Brienz, you will see, from a good way off, a knot of pretty girls waiting at their ease for travellers to appear. On approaching you will hear them singing: beautiful and strange melodies sung by lilting, joyful voices. They sing for the favours of the passengers they row across

to the Giessbach Falls. Gay young women in folk costumes, who will turn the head of any young English-man of strict upbringing and make it difficult for him to choose a boat at all.

The loveliest of these lovely ferrywomen is Elisabeth Grossmann, also known as "La Belle Batelière". Plays are written about her, and her beauty extolled in song all over Europe. She becomes the girl of every young traveller's dreams. Hers is the beauty idealized in every salon. Her praises are still being sung long after her marriage to a luckless innkeeper. And she still dwells in men's dreams long after

poverty and despair have befallen her. Rumour has it that she is to be seen begging on the streets of Grindelwald. An English touring party may notice her slumped on the church steps and one of them remark: "This was once La Belle Batelière, the loveliest boatwoman of Brienz."

Act 3: **The Adornment of Paradise.**

Perhaps, like Hegel and Goethe, you had other expectations of your long-awaited encounter with paradise. The phenomenon is known to all of us: one dreams a dream and yearns to have it come true. And when it finally does, it is unrecognizable. But paradise was not invented for the sake of philosophers. It was created for the fashionable people of a century ago, ready to swoon at the drop of a hat. The stage was conjured up for their benefit, and for them it must now be set. The buildings that go up really are like stage sets: sumptuous baroque and renaissance palaces, with arabesque towers, straight out of a fairy tale. The stage is set in the Theatre of the Alps, the actors can begin their play: five changes of clothes a day – evening gown and tails for the visit to a lamp-lit glacier. The frissons and swooning, the "excitation bizarre" must be made as comfortable as possible.

Whoever was responsible for the decor at Monte Carlo really knew what furnishing and fitting paradise was all about: high society must feel as unconstrained there as they would at court. The members of the upper middle class must be made to feel like the aristocracy.

The first palaces are built at Interlaken, facing the Eiger, Mönch and Jungfrau, and within striking distance of the Giessbach Falls.

The architects of paradise grow more daring. Only a bold visionary would take international high society at its word by building a palace on a moraine of the Rhone glacier.

Rousseau it was who evoked the state when one "soars above the human sojourn".

Villeneuve
L'Embouchure du Rhône
Bouveret
St Gingolph
Les Rochers de Meillerie.

Engelmann pi

L'HOT

Ses Bain

La te

BYRON.

Minérale.
ra

Le Château de Chillon
Montreux
Le Château du Chatelard
Clarens Vevey
La Tour de Gourze
Lausanne

Beside the lake that cost Julie her life, the lake evoked by Byron, you can now while away a few days during the season with quiet boating parties and noisy balls in the most refined company.

135

You can dine beside the surging, boiling, hissing, roaring Rhine Falls. And take in the spectacle from the best vantage point without getting your feet wet. You may also contemplate the spectacle by nocturnal illuminations if you so desire.

Isn't this what palaces look like when you dream of palaces? And do they not stand in Caux, with Lake Geneva lapping at their ramparts?

Or does it look like St. Moritz when you close your eyes and try to imagine a palace?

LARGEST STEAME

Hotels shoot up on lakesides and mountain slopes, on peaks and in gorges, in the most remote and

vertiginous corners of paradise. They seem as alien and forlorn, as strangely aloof as the huge ocean

RS IN THE WORLD

liners, which glide by in the still of the night, a world unto themselves.

Would you have recognized Lucerne, having seen it through the eyes of Queen Victoria? The lakeside has come to resemble the quay at Monte Carlo. By no means an accident, for the Hotel National, which is considered Europe's finest, is managed by that paragon of hoteliers César Ritz. And the chef de cuisine is none other than the great Escoffier. Both are to be found in Monte Carlo during the winter season.

No well-appointed paradise is complete without special attractions. So it is no surprise to learn that Lucerne has its own diorama where you can marvel at the Alpine skyline without first having to

climb the Rigi. There is also a glacier park where the Alpine world can be viewed at your leisure, between luncheon and thé dansant – no need to exhaust yourself with all that tiresome tramping about.

Not everybody is as daring a mountaineer as Byron's Manfred. But bold feats of engineering put the marvels of paradise within everybody's reach. The showplaces of the act of evocation can be visited with a minimum of effort. A cable railway scales the giddy heights of the Wetterhorn.

Dark tunnels open out onto breath-taking panoramas, such as this one on the Jungfrau.

Giessbach and St. Moritz have been turned into holiday resorts in which everything is planned down to the very last detail: vast and costly amusement parks for the most sophisticated first-class travellers.

LEGENDE

1. Piz Julier
2. Piz Albana
3. Piz Polaschin
4. Lac de Sils et Silvaplana
5. Oberalpina
6. Route vers Campfer
7. Villas
8. Villa Concordia
9. Villa Gruneberg
10. Tour penchante
11. Gd Hotel Engadiner Kulm
12. Palace Hotel

13. Grand Hotel
14. Private Hotel
15. Hotel Caspar Badrutt
16. Patinage Suedois
17. Rink du Palace-Hotel
18. Rink du Curvercin
19. Village Run
20. Bobsleigh p.apprendre
21. Gulley Run p.apprendre
22. Route au bord du Lac
23. Route vers le chemin de fer
24. Curling Rink

25. Grd Kulm Rink
26. Petit-Kulm Rink
27. Curling Rink
28. Route à Cresta-Pontresina
29. Cresta-Run
30. Route à travers Badrutts Park
31. Bobsleigh Run
32. Ski Run
33. Hockey Rink
34. Gare du chemin de fer Rhetique
35. Fleuve de l'In
36. Ligne de chemin de fer vers Celerina-Samaden

The paradise that has been fabricated bears little resemblance to the paradise that was evoked at the beginning of our story. To achieve success on an international scale it had to be tailored to the needs of European high society – people whose lives were dedicated to preening themselves in public. One does not enter a restaurant or dining room because one is hungry and wishes to eat, but because one is due on stage. And for a stage appearance one expects the accustomed scenery and props.

Nor does one wish to forgo the pleasures of the casino. Not even among the firs at Waldhaus Flims.

This is an adornment worthy of paradise. The Maloja Palace on the banks of the Lake of Sils, where northern and southern Europe meet, a half-way house between Monte Carlo and Baden-Baden. This vast palace is the greatest of all the great profanities in paradise. It has a casino, ballrooms, a theatre, a

One expects sumptuous evenings in the whirling ballrooms. All the better if they are held on ice. One can dance oneself giddy on ice, dance until the world goes down.

concert hall and 700 beds for the Russian nobility and their retinues. On fine afternoons you can take tea in the newly built ruins of a mediaeval castle to the sound of the Scala orchestra, the musicians' fingers numbed by the Maloja wind.

And what parties they throw at Maloja! The "Soirée vénitienne", for example. Gondolas, brought specially from Venice, are adorned in festive manner and fitted with tables and chairs. To guard against inclement weather and avoid the ladies' having to wrap themselves up in warm clothes, the floating restaurant is not launched on the Lake of Sils but in the main dining room, flooded for the occasion. The damage will be extensive; but Count Renaisse, who finances the hotel, is very, very rich. And we know of his ambition to make the Maloja Palace the casino between Monte Carlo and Baden-Baden. To the sound of mandolins, the brightly-lit gondolas glide through the glittering dining room. With a fleet of smaller buffet boats in attendance, the dinner guests, or passengers, are served exquisite Venetian specialities. Outside, behind the heavy curtains, snow is falling.

10178 Trabfahre

That St. Moritz enjoys an exceptional climate, even in the cold season, was never in any doubt. And that several metres of snow is the icing on the cake of paradise is something we have known since Byron. But we did entertain doubts about the short winter days: would we not find them a crushing bore.

But an English gentleman worth his salt is never bored. And what amusements they invented: toboggan races in which a brace of men are steered by a fearless lady. Or eggblowing on ice. Or horse races in which each rider pulls two ladies on skis. Or cricket on ice. Jolly good fun.

Birds of a feather.

Act 4: **Life in Paradise.**

We have seen how paradise was evoked, encountered and accoutered. The oft-invoked aborigines of paradise, the legendary heroes of Helvetian independence have developed an inimitable talent for anticipating the luxury traveller's every wish, and creating, with a meticulous eye for detail, the surroundings in which these dreams, however modest or exalted, can be made to come true. Paradise is in vogue. Among those who flock to its door are the false princes, demi-mondaines, hotel thieves, bridge teachers and gigolos; but there are also the emperors, kings, geniuses, demi-gods and stars with whom they mingle. There is life in paradise.

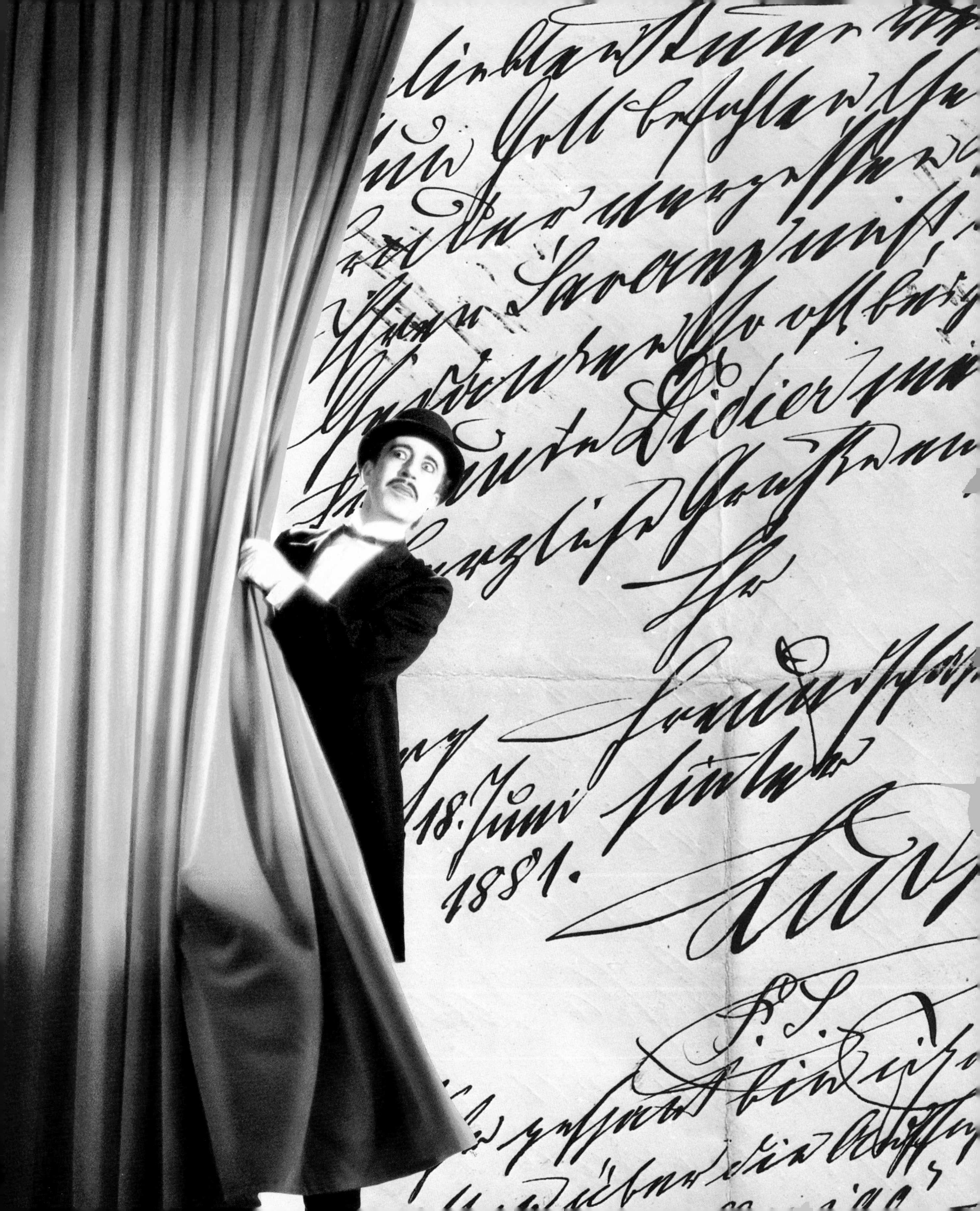
18. Juni
1881.

This is a letter written by the most bizarre crowned head of the last century to a young artist who was destined to become the most celebrated actor of his day. What follows is the incredible (but true) story of a journey into paradise.

Louis II, the King of Bavaria, had fairy-tale castles built all over his kingdom, far away from his subjects, with whom he increasingly lost touch. A favourite pastime was to visit the Residenz Theatre where special performances were given for his benefit behind closed doors. In May 1881 Victor Hugo's tale of the demi-monde, "Marion de Lorme", is put on. The king is captivated by the performance of Josef Kainz as the foundling, Didier, who dies on Richelieu's gallows beside his friend the Marquis de Saverny.

After the performance, Louis sends the handsome actor a ring of sapphires and diamonds. Kainz is summoned to Schloss Linderhof where the king receives him in a Venus grotto illuminated by Bengal lights. They dine in a floating, silver shell. An orchestrina plays excerpts from Rossini's Tell. Louis suggests to Kainz, who is shortly to play Melchtal in a Munich staging of Schiller's Tell, that they journey together to Switzerland. Here, at the scene of the drama, the actor might "allow his very body to be penetrated by the character he is to play".

One month later they set off on their journey, the king travelling as the Marquis de Saverny, Kainz as Didier. Thus disguised and with a retinue of twelve servants, they board a special train for Lucerne. But of course, they are recognized wherever they go. Near Lucerne they transfer to a steamer which carries them to Brunnen. They are greeted by a crowd of curious onlookers. It is all up with their romantic incognito – they do not break their journey but continue directly to the Tell shrine. They obtain a view of the half-finished fresco depicting the apple and crossbow scene. The painter, Stückelberg, falls from grace when he confuses the two guests, mistakenly addressing Kainz as "Your Majesty".

They steam to and fro on the Lake of Lucerne for a long time until forced to land at Brunnen. The King is under the impression that the Axenschloss has been reserved for him before the departure from Munich. As it turns out, he only has a floor of the Grand Hotel Axenstein at his disposal. His disgust is compounded by the reception committee: a guard of honour formed by the waiters, hotel guests and officious gendarmes.

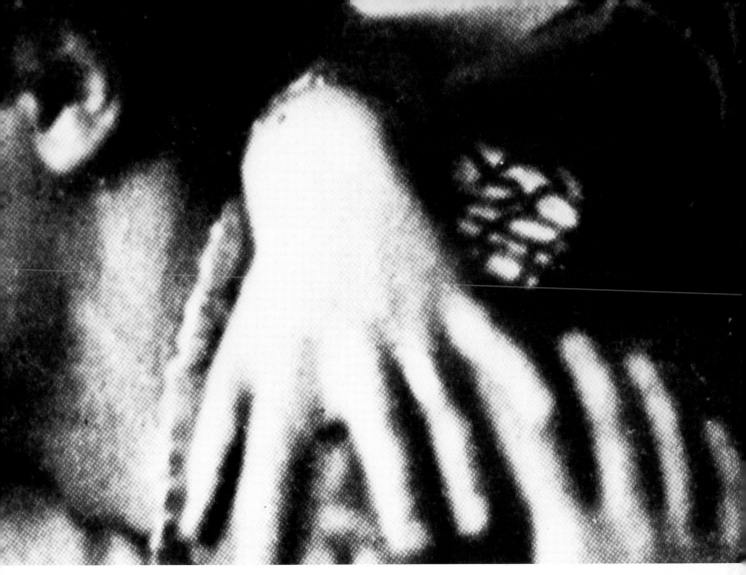

Louis moves into the Villa Gutenberg at Mythenstein with his young hero. They are now on familiar terms and over a glass of wine Louis bemoans the burden of responsibility weighing on him. In this relaxed mood, Kainz suggests he hand the crown to someone else if he has become weary of it. Louis delivers a sharp rebuff for this "tasteless jest". The following day Kainz begs forgiveness: "It was an ill-considered remark – the wine went to my head; one forgets oneself so easily when drinking wine." Louis offers his hand in a gesture of conciliation, saying: "I love wine, even when it overflows – and that was all that happened yesterday." Kainz is disconcerted, uncertain how to behave towards his eccentric benefactor, who worships and fetters him at the same time. Later Kainz says of his stay in paradise: "I could have put up with anything if he had only let me sleep."

You will understand his despair in a moment:

Almost daily, Kainz is obliged to visit the Rütli by landau and steamer. He must declaim his speeches from Tell by moonlight. The first time, he finds it a fascinating experience. But after several repetitions he becomes bored and tries to smuggle passages from Tasso and Hamlet into the role. But the king will have none of it. He is tireless in his determination to be held in thrall over and over again by the same scene: "Let me weep, let me shed scalding tears on thy breast, my only friend!" He drags Kainz round every single place

where the action is set, getting him to recite the appropriate passages: Altdorf for the apple shot; Gessler's death in the Hohle Gasse, the Kaiser's death before the ruins of Burg Zwing-Uri in Altdorf, Tell's parting from his wife at Hedwig's house in Bürglen. He even obliges Kainz to follow Melchtal on his exhausting march "over the cruel heights of Surennen." The king, for whom the trek is far too strenuous, is waiting at the finish. In the same night, Louis drags Kainz, for the umpteenth time, to Tell's shrine and the Rütli.

The moon is full. Fourteen alphorn players serenade them during the journey until they get too loud for Louis and he sets them ashore at Brunnen. Kainz has fallen into an exhausted sleep. They reach the Rütli at three in the morning and Louis insists on a repetition of the Melchtal scene. Kainz refuses, and when the king becomes insistent, he throws himself to the ground in utter despair. Louis returns, deeply offended, to the landing stage, leaving Kainz behind. The friendship is over.

On the following day they meet in Lucerne for the last time. They visit a photographer's and have their picture taken. Kainz comments: "...like His Majesty's Moorish bodyguard, so black, so foolish the expression, so like an African chieftain in posture".

And the King of Bavaria opines: "Our sojourn in Switzerland lies behind me like a dream, wrought of conflicting memories, both pleasant and disagreeable."

They journey back to Munich together by train as far as the border. Then they part – forever.

But it is a different story when the crowned heads of Europe pay an official visit to Lucerne. The date is 2nd May, 1893. The Hotel National has been spruced up in expectation of the German Kaiser and Kaiserin.

The quay is packed with sightseers who have been waiting for hours beneath a sea of waving flags. The more fortunate have taken to the water in boats. It is 9.57. The imperial steamship docks. Hip hip hooray.

The imperial couple crosses the quay in dignified manner and...

...disappears inside the Schweizerhof where a banquet is waiting. An address by the President of the Confederation, a concert, little girls in traditional dress. Outside, the crowds wait.

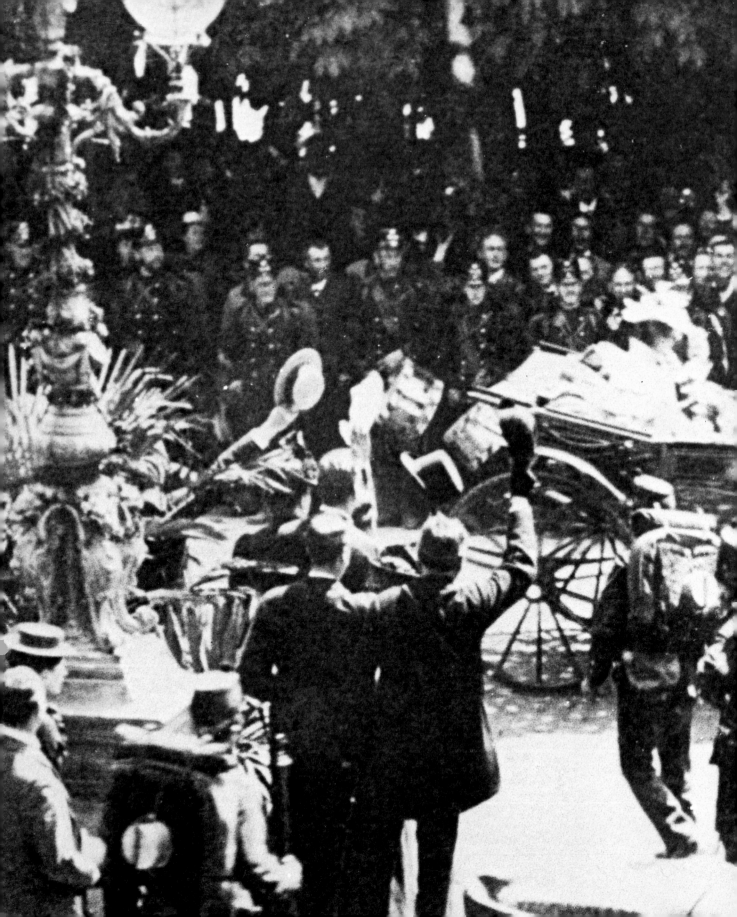

A few hours later the doors swing open and a carriage draws away bearing the royal guests to the station. Hooray, hooray. And they are gone.

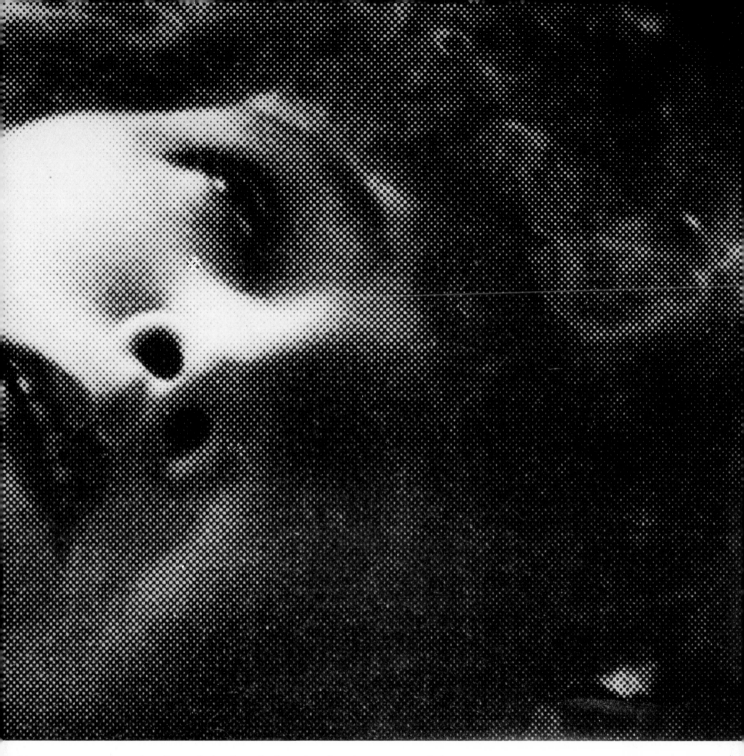

No, you are not mistaken. It is Sarah Bernhardt, the most celebrated tragedienne of the century. Is this goddess to play before half empty theatres in the European capitals, forsaken by her audience for the delights of the high season in paradise? When her great rival, La Duse, is not above making guest appearances in paradise?

Sarah Bernhardt has just arrived at the Lucerne National. The hotel is under the management of César Ritz, the Valaisan shepherd boy, the king of the hoteliers and hotelier to the kings.

Sarah Bernhardt is notorious for her moodiness and tantrums. It is said of her that she play-acts 24 hours a day.

Madame Sarah is due on stage in the restaurant. She is led to her table by César Ritz himself. In the dining room a nervous 18-year-old waiter from Grisons is at the ready. He has been chosen as her personal waiter because of his fluent French.

She soon gives the other guests something to gape at. The young waiter is summoned to her table and Sarah explains at some length that she is accustomed to having her place laid in precisely the same way at every meal: the salt here, the sugar there, the wine glass here, and so on. She is in the habit of reading while she eats and does not want to have to grope for things on the table. And, she adds sternly, I shall tell you once and once only.

Every day she is to be seen at table reading her newspaper. From time to time a hand appears from behind the paper to fasten securely on one of the objects set out before her in the desired pattern. All is well. Of the waiter she takes not the slightest notice.

One day the young waiter is caught fooling around with a colleague at the serving table. He is summarily dismissed. In complete despair he goes to his attic room to pack his belongings. Suddenly, the manager of the restaurant bursts in and orders him back to the dining room. You can guess what has happened. Sarah, unaware of the fate that has befallen her waiter, reaches from behind her newspaper for the salt. Her hand closes on the sugar. She raises her eyes for the first time, sees an unfamiliar figure at her elbow and explodes. She screams through the stunned silence of the dining room for her waiter, whom Ritz has fired. The breath-taking, impromptu offering of her theatrical genius does not end until the waiter has been reinstated. His job and probably his career in the hotel trade is saved.

One evening, our diva is so intoxicated by the ovation she receives at the end of her performance that she cannot bring herself to leave the stage. The little waiter is kept waiting so long that he falls asleep in a chair, exhausted by fourteen hours on his feet. Hush now, we are about to witness a moment of pure magic. Sarah sweeps into the deserted dining room, sees the sleeping youth and bends over him. He is startled awake and begins to stammer an excuse. But she is smiling down at him, such a smile that his head begins to spin, and she tells him how glad she is that he waited. And then? ...she kisses his brow.

It is high time that I introduce a man who, though critical of the high life in paradise, did not allow his outraged conscience to divert him from his enjoyment of its pleasures.

Better still, I will let him tell the story in his own words: "When the chronicle of our times comes to be written, the incident I am about to relate should be inscribed in letters of everlasting fire. This event is of greater significance and gravity, and has a deeper meaning than all the facts recorded in our history books and newspapers."

In the summer of 1857, long before "War and Peace", "Anna Karenina", the Nobel Prize and world renown, Tolstoy goes on a tour of Switzerland:

"I arrived in Lucerne yesterday evening and booked in at the best hotel, the Schweizerhof. (...) I went up to my room and on opening the window that looks out onto the lake I was quite literally dazzled and shaken for a moment by the beauty of the scene before me – the lake, the mountains and the sky. A sense of unease came over me, the need to express in some way that which filled my soul almost to bursting. In that moment I was seized by the desire to clasp somebody, anybody, in my arms, to embrace them tightly, to tickle or even pinch them, and generally do something quite outrageous to them or to myself."

"Dinner was announced at half past seven. In the large and sumptuously furnished ground-floor restaurant two long tables were laid for at least a hundred people. It took about three minutes for all the guests to appear. Hardly a word was spoken as they forgathered: the only sounds were the rustle of the ladies' gowns, the padding footsteps and muted exchanges with the elegantly dressed waiters whose manner was uncommonly courteous. (...) As everywhere in Switzerland, a majority of the

guests were English; accordingly, the tone at the table d'hôte was determined by a strict code of etiquette, a reserve not born of a sense of pride, but of the guests' complete disinclination to have anything whatever to do with their fellows. (...) Indeed, in many faces one can read only a feeling of complacency and an utter lack of interest in anything that does not directly concern them."

"When two of these hundred people do converse, it is a safe bet that their talk is of the weather – or of climbing the Rigi." (Considering the different views above, it is little wonder that everyone speaks differently of the same thing.)

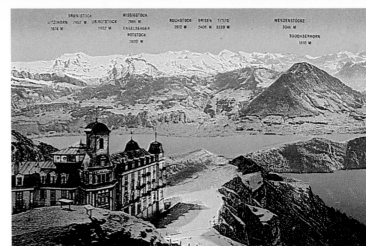

Rigi-Kulm mit Nebelmeer und Pilatus

Rigi-Kulm

1324. Rigi Kulm mit den Bemeralpen

Why this sudden unrest in the wings? Forgive me, honoured members of the public, if I do not stick to the letter of Tolstoy's text. But there are some important actors in our spectacle impatient to get on stage.

"At the end of the meal I was overcome with sadness; I left my dessert, rose from the table and went out into the streets feeling rather grumpy." The sight of "women in superior hats, scurrying down the street, keeping close to the walls and looking repeatedly about them, did nothing to dispel my mood of gloom, indeed, it only deepened. (...) As I crossed the quay, looking neither right nor left, to regain the Schweizerhof, I was suddenly aware of strange, yet pleasant music which held me in its thrall. (...) It was as though a bright and joyful light had pierced the shadows about my soul. (...) The beauty of the night and the lake, of which I had been oblivious a moment before, was borne in upon me as though it were entirely new."

"I looked in the direction from which the music was coming and saw in the half-light a small crowd which had gathered in a semi-circle a few paces from a small figure dressed all in black. The soft, sensuous chords of his guitar, the charm of the simple melody and the lonely figure of the black-clad musician in the midst of that fantastic scenery (...) – it was uncanny, yet indescribably lovely, or so it seemed to me. (...) It was as though a sweetly scented flower had opened in my soul."

Three times the singer ceases his playing and addresses the listeners gathered around him or looking

down from the balcony of the hotel: "Ladies and Gentlemen, if you imagine that I earn a sou like this, you are mistaken, for I am a miserable wretch." Apart from a little laughter, his appeal elicits not the slightest response. The fine ladies and gentlemen draw back from the windows and balconies talking quietly amongst themselves, and the small musician makes off quickly. "I felt an immediate sympathy for this poor fellow, and was grateful for the change of humour he had brought me."

Tolstoy, burning with indignation at the callousness of his fellow guests, goes back into the hotel for a short while. Then, he sets out again to seek the street-singer. Soon tracking him down, he bids him share a bottle of wine at the hotel. To his astonishment, he is refused entry to the dining room and shown instead to the public bar, set aside for the common people. Instead of bowing and scraping as is their wont, the staff serve him sullenly, with scarcely suppressed sneers. He is so incensed that he forces

his way into the dining room and sits down with his guest at a table near the only two remaining diners. These rise immediately huffing in indignation and leave the room. The singer, by this time quite intimidated, drinks up quickly and stammers his thanks. Tolstoy accompanies him proudly through the hall, past the flunkeys and porters, and takes leave of his guest with all the proper courtesies. Back in his room, he draws unexpected conclusions from his experience:

"How is such a thing possible, here, where civilization, liberty and equality have brought forth their most perfect flower, where the most highly cultured representatives of the most highly cultured nations meet? In the deathly hush of the darkened streets I heard the little singer play, and I said to myself: No, you have no right to pity him nor to condemn the lord for his wealth. Who has weighed the joys and sorrows that dwell in the innermost souls of these men? Boundless is the goodness and wisdom of Him who has permitted and commanded such contradictions."

No not you, Heidi! I did want to take our audience to the Engadine, but it isn't you they're interested in – certainly not in your adult life, anyway. Yes, I know the whole world was fascinated by the story of your youth; but your sixty years as a chambermaid at the "Palace" won't interest a soul. This is most embarassing! Curtain. C u r t a i n !

Ladies and Gentlemen, please accept my apologies: you realize what it's like with these childstars of yesteryear... Old Heidi feels she was rather exploited by that Johanna Spyri. Taken to the bottle a bit, I'm afraid. Thank you for being such an understanding audience. Curtain!

Now, this is the place I wanted to show you. The area in which Friedrich Nietzsche spent nine summers of his life: Sils Maria, between the "eyes of Engadine" as the philosopher liked to call the twin lakes of Upper Engadine.

Between 1880 and 1888 Nietzsche is a regular summer visitor, inhabiting a room belonging to the mayor Herr Durisch. It is sparsely furnished and the only window opens onto a wall of rock. His daily round is as regular as clockwork: After a frugal breakfast which he prepares himself, he works for six hours without a break. Lunch is taken at the "Hotel Edelweiss". He eats alone and always orders steak and peas. He shuns all company and will suffer no intrusion on his privacy. A persistent autograph huntress obliges him to change from the "Edelweiss" to the "Alpenrose" in the final summer. Every day after lunch he takes the same walk: Across the meadows between the lakes to the hamlet Chasté from which the valley known as Fextal opens out. His host, Herr Durisch, is his constant, and silent, companion. Nietzsche has asked him to remain a few paces behind. During the walks Nietzsche gesticulates a lot

230

and holds loud conversations with himself. Now and again he halts abruptly and begins to sing loudly to the open countryside.

After the walk he continues with his work. In Sils Maria Nietzsche is seized by the idea of eternal recurrence, the kernel of his most celebrated work "Thus spoke Zarathustra". In "Ecce Homo" he writes: "The basic conception of the work, the idea of eternal recurrence, the highest formula of affirmation that can possibly be attained – belongs to the August of the year 1881: it was jotted down on a piece of paper with the inscription: '6,000 feet beyond man and time'. I was that day walking through the woods beside the lake of Silvaplana; I stopped beside a mighty pyramidal block of stone which reared itself up not far from Surlej. Then this idea came to me."

Triebschen! Twenty-three times Nietzsche visited the house on the headland at the foot of Mount Pilatus. It is the home of someone who in his own lifetime has become a tourist attraction in paradise. However much I might tell of the occupants of this villa, it could never suffice. Only this: the "Island of the

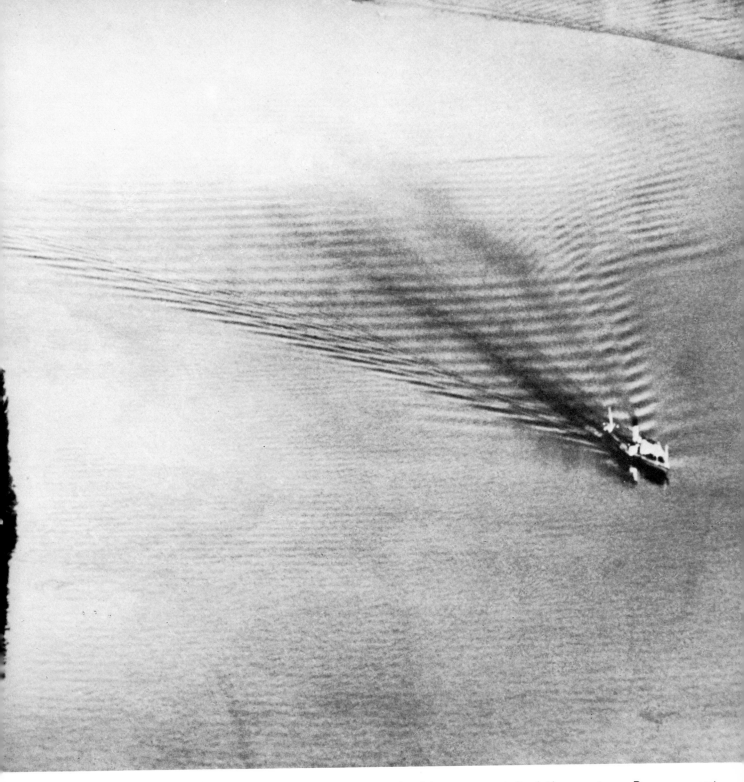

Blessed" is the home of Richard and Cosima Wagner, the "dream couple" of the century. Do you want to know what Wagner thinks of his union with Cosima? Would you like to get a close-up of the scene? Well, alright. But only for a moment:

"Only once in every 3,000 years are two such as we given to meet." His very own words: Who would wish to intrude?

Act 5: **The End of Paradise.**

I promised, at the beginning, that I would guide you back to the solid ground of reality. And the time has now come. But I shall not lead you out of paradise; I shall, instead, lead paradise to its end. Have no fear: it will not end with a whimper but a roar; an eccentric, dramatic and – to say the least – stylish exit. I have given you the evocation, the encounter, the adornment and the lifestyle. Now I give you The Finale.

Two men are locked in a grim and silent struggle. The glow of Bengal torches reveals a slippery wall of rock behind them, reflecting on the lean features of an impassive countenance. What is hidden in the dark wells of those eyes? Is it fiery resolution? Or calm resignation?

One of them is loosing his balance. Or both? The ledge is so narrow, the rock so slippery. Let go! No! They're going to drag one another into the abyss. Are they over? Did they... Now! They plunge over the edge, the wind drawing a fine curtain of spray over the scene. When it blows away again, the two figures have vanished from sight. All that remains is the deafening roar of the Reichenbach Falls and the play of Bengal light, which illuminates the spectacle at night for the benefit of tourists.

You have just witnessed the end of the greatest detective the world has ever seen: Sherlock Holmes. Wearying of his sisyphean struggle against the dull and ordinary, he has sought a confrontation: a dangerous duel with Moriarty, the "Napoleon of Crime". As a setting for this fateful combat he has chosen the "gigantic, titanic scenery of the Alps". Holmes has just arrived, in the guise of an Italian priest, with an appointment to meet his good friend Dr Watson in Interlaken. But throughout his journey he has been unable to shake off the feeling of being watched, and he is not in the least bit surprised when Watson is called back to the hotel from the foot of the Reichenbach Falls, apparently to attend an injured person. Holmes senses that somewhere in the tortuous ravine, Moriarty is lying in wait. He pushes on undaunted.

Holmes dead? It is unthinkable. Just look at the throng of admirers, jostling to get a look at the illuminated scene of his demise. And Conan Doyle, Holmes' creator, is not unmoved by this display of devotion. The great detective is resurrected. In the bedside table of Holmes' room at his hotel, a number of unpublished manuscripts are discovered.

Since 30th August 1898 an eminent guest has been staying with her retinue at the Grand Hotel de Caux: Elisabeth, the restless, nervy and highly sensitive Empress of Austria, obsessed with beauty and with death. Since her only son Rudolph, the successor to the throne, took his life at Mayerling, she has wandered Europe like a wraith, a black-clad figure, drifting between Bad Kissingen, the Aegean, Spain, Tunisia, Sicily, Portugal, Turkey and Lake Leman. She seldom visits Vienna. To her husband, Kaiser Franz Josef, who idolizes her like an unattainable and unrequited love, she addresses barely a word. She won't, and he can't. Elisabeth is 61. Quite tall at 172 cm, she has starved herself down to a meagre

46 kilos, and at the slightest sign of gaining weight she plunges into a deep depression which lasts for several days. She speaks without moving her lips to hide the stumps of rotten teeth – the merest shadow of the most beautiful woman in Europe she once was. Using fans and little parasols to hide her face, she has shunned the photographers for years. But we might just be in luck. If our man were to get to the other side of the lake... The Kaiserin is going on a trip to Geneva, travelling incognito, of course, as the Countess of Hohenembs. Alas, the hotel management has indiscreetly disclosed her arrival to the society columns of the press.

And here she is at last. With her lady companion Irma Sztaray. This photographic document cost a good deal of patience. The imperial party arrived in Geneva yesterday and went straight to Pregny to call on Countess Julie de Rothschild. Toward evening, Elisabeth retired to her hotel room for an hour. Then we just missed seeing her at the Confiserie Désanod. Night was falling by the time she reached the premises of Dunier, cabinet-makers, to choose a table with marquetry work for Archduchess Valérie. Later, the town was plunged into darkness by a power cut. The Empress and her companion were obliged to find their way back to the hotel

by torchlight. Elisabeth is unable to sleep for the noise of street-singers, the constantly changing colours of the lighthouse and the glaring moon. But today, 10th September, we finally get our surreptitious photographs of the two ladies. Her Majesty has just bought an orchestrina with 24 rolls from the well known music shop Bäcker, and now she hurries along the pavement with her companion. At twenty minutes to two her steamer is due to sail back to Territet. How fortunate that our photographer had the patience to wait long enough. But what a great misfortune that a certain other person showed the same perseverance.

Isn't that Irma Sztaray on the Quai du Mont Blanc? But why the look of horror on her face? We'll ask her: "I saw, at some distance, near the hotel where the carriages stand, a man making towards us. He ran across the pavement to the railings of the lakeside promenade, then he turned on his heel and ran straight towards us. He seemed to stumble, then lurched forward and in a single movement struck the Empress a blow with his fist."

S. M. L'IMPÉRATRICE ELISABETH D'AUTRICHE

Here, we see what the European picture press made of the drama. You can even read for yourself the assassin's own description of his deed: "I didn't want to get the wrong one, they both wore black. I recognized her. She wasn't as beautiful as all that, getting on a bit already. I knew she would die as soon as I'd stabbed her. I put all my strength behind it and felt the blade go in deep." The words of Luigi Luccheni, aged 26. He offers no resistance when they arrest him. He is laughing and demands the death penalty (which has already been abolished in Geneva). Luccheni is an individualistic anarchist who shuns all forms of organization. His dream is to rise above the mass by committing a political murder. His makeshift weapon consists of a rusty file with a rough wooden handle. Originally, he planned to assassinate Prince Henri d'Orléans who is staying in the area. But, on learning that the Empress of Austria is in Geneva, he decides to make her his victim instead.

Luigi is arrested at the scene of the crime. The Empress gets to her feet with the aid of a porter who has rushed over from the hotel. She retrieves her fan and her sun-shade, and, after a friendly word of greeting to the gathering crowd, continues on her way to the landing stage. The incident has given her a shock; she feels a pain in her chest, but is not sure what to make of it. "She walked before me with a light step on the gangway, but hardly had she set foot on board than she halted, gasping: 'Quick, give me your arm!'" Then she slides unconscious to the floor. The ship is already underway. The Empress is carried to the upper deck. Someone sprinkles her with eau de Cologne and puts a sugar cube dipped in

ether between her teeth. "The Kaiserin opened her eyes slowly and lay for a few minutes, her eyes darting to and fro as though she were trying to get her bearings. Then she raised herself slowly to a sitting position. Her eyes sought the sky, then settled on the Dents du Midi. 'What has befallen me now?' Her last words, as it proved. Then she fell back in a faint." Irma opens the tight bands of her black silk costume and discovers, in the region of the heart, a small triangular wound which is barely bleeding. The steamer turns back towards Geneva. The dying Empress is carried back to her hotel room on an improvised stretcher. At twenty minutes to three a doctor pronounces her dead.

At the Hotel Beau-Rivage the shutters have been drawn down. The Empress is lying in state in a corner salon. The correspondent of the Neue Zürcher Zeitung reports: "I have just left the Kaiserin's death-bed. She is lying in state in a corner room on the first floor. The coffin is open and draped with a white lace shroud which bears the words 'Repose en Paix'. Through this flimsy veil, which entirely covers the body, the peaceful features of the deceased are visible. The catafalque is encircled with huge

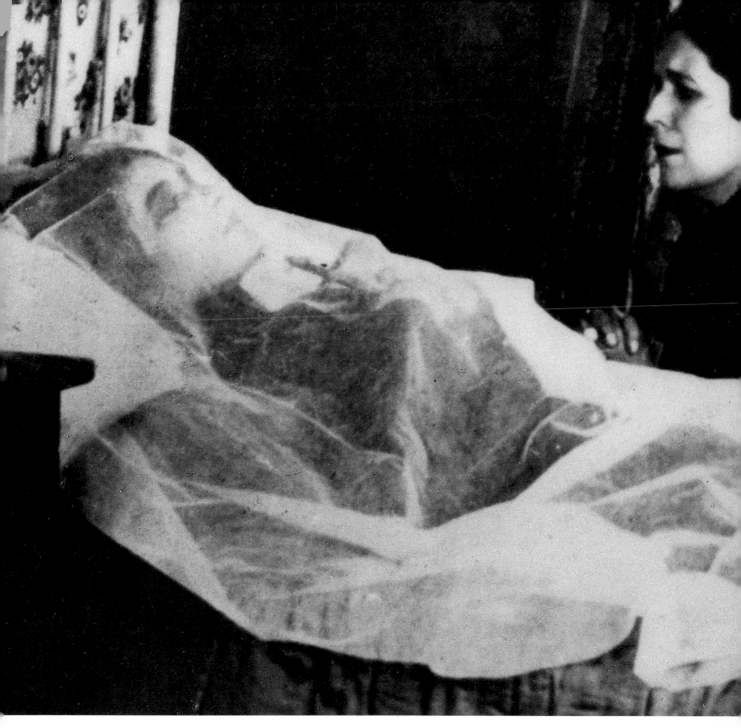

candles in silver candelabra. There are palms in every corner of the room. Priests keep up a constant murmur of prayer. So many are the wreaths and flowers that only a handful of mourners can squeeze in. On the broad ribbon in the Swiss national colours of red and white that is closest to the pall, the follow-ing words can be made out: 'Hommage du Conseil Fédéral au nom du peuple Suisse'."

In Territet, near the old cable railway to Caux, there is a monument to the beautiful empress, showing her in the bloom of youth she wished to retain forever. In her testament she decrees that her poems are

À LA MÉMOIRE DE

SA MAJESTÉ L'IMPERATRICE ET REINE ELISABETH

to be published, the proceeds to go to those "unhappy souls who, because of their love of freedom, have been branded as criminals".

In the testament Luigi Luccheni leaves to a stunned world are the words: "If the ruling classes do not cease to suck the blood of their fellow men, they will suffer, in quick succession, a series of blows such as that inflicted by the undersigned. And not only the aristocracy, the presidents and government ministers shall be struck down, but all who seek to profit from the oppression of their fellow men.

260

The day is not far when the true friends of mankind shall erase all that has been written in the annals. A single sentence shall suffice the builders of a new world: Chi non lavora non mangia. He who does not work shall not eat.

Yours in solidarity, Luigi Luccheni, wholly convinced anarchist."

And now, the hotel that was indiscreet enough to break the incognito of the Countess of Hohenembs, must suffer an indiscretion on my part. The truth must out, Ladies and Gentlemen: the management of the Beau-Rivage actually sent the bill for Elisabeth's last meal to Vienna.

...isserie

...mmet pain

2 Consommés   2 25

1 filet pommes   5 2

1 Viande f... frites   1

1 Sirop limonade   2

2 Soda ½   3 25

1 Villeneuve Médoc   4 50

2 V. Rhum   1 20

3 Soupers dment   3 75

3 Déjeuners app   2 50

thés spl   1   9 — 27 2 35

lait spl 1 œufs c   6

viande carte app   4 50

...res carte   1 25

   36

...n et sel   5 6

   15

   5

   3

The Belle Epoque lasts a few short years more. A political assassination then occurs which is to signal its end: in Sarajevo, far away from paradise and yet so close, the successor to the Austrian throne and his wife are slain by an anarchist. Within the space of a few days the birds of paradise have all flown home: to Berlin, London, Paris, St. Petersburg and Vienna. And everywhere the picture is the same:

In London, the Foreign Secretary Lord Grey says: "The lamps are going out all over Europe; we shall not see them lit again in our lifetime."

The only visitors to remain in paradise are a few consumptives who can afford to stay on. They lie through the long nights on the terraces of their sanatoria, breathing the pure mountain air...

...and doze through the day, wrapped up in blankets, high above the sea of fog, under the healing sun. Otherwise, there remain but a handful of outsiders. I have engaged one of their number for the Grand Finale:

Waslaw Nijinsky, the greatest dancer of all time, is waiting in paradise for the catastrophe to end. His only company consists of a few sorry emigrés who maintain the luxurious lifestyle to which they are accustomed until the last gold spoon in their baggage has been sold.

It is the winter of 1918; the war is over. Nijinsky and his wife have rented the Villa Guardamunt in St. Moritz. A favourite meeting place after tobogganing is the Konditorei Hanselmann. Or in the evenings

at one of the many spiritualists for a table-lifting session. Nijinsky is causing his wife Romola much distress: He wears a heavy golden cross on his breast and stops strangers on the street to enquire whether they have been to mass yet. Everywhere he goes he sees traces of blood in the snow. The madness of war has left him paralyzed with horror. He has not danced in public for over two years.

One day, the pianist Berta Felber pays them a visit and persuades Nijinsky to give a benefit performance for the Red Cross at Suvretta House. On his insistence there are no rehearsals; they simply drive to the Suvretta towards evening. Nijinsky broods in silence during the sleigh-ride. Romola asks him what she should tell the pianist to play when she has no idea what he wants to dance. "I will tell her when the time comes. Do not speak now, be still. Today is the day of my wedding with God."

The dining hall of the Suvretta is crowded with about 200 people. It is cool inside owing to the coal shortage. The guests wait. Then Nijinsky appears on stage. He takes a chair and sits facing the audience, staring at them. Silence. Ten minutes pass. Then fifteen. Berta Felber plays the opening bars of the

"Sylphides", then the "Spectre". At last Nijinsky comes to life, moving his hands in time to the music, each sound embodied by a movement of its own. Until he stops, abruptly, places his hands over his heart and intones in a loud voice; "The little horse is weary." The audience is getting very restless. Some rise to leave.

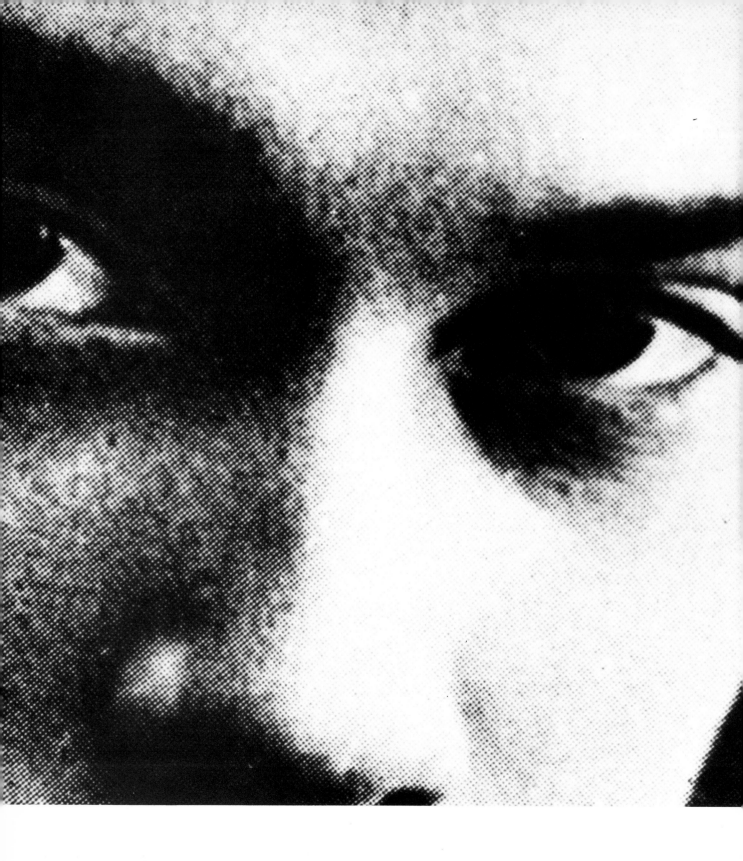

Nijinsky stands. He takes some black fabric from the stage decorations and fashions a huge cross on the parquet. Then he begins to dance. For the last time in his life.

We witness once again his breath-taking dance style, the fantastic pirouettes, the astonishing leaps, defying Nature's laws, the inexplicable standing-still-in-midair. He stops suddenly and stands in the centre of the cross. He raises his arms, becoming himself a living cross, and remains thus for a moment. "And now, Ladies and Gentlemen, war will come. I will dance the war for you, war, devastation and death.

The war you did not prevent, and for which you are responsible."

A deathly hush. Nobody moves. Frau Felber strikes up a march. Nijinsky's expression changes abruptly.

High up at the zenith of a leap, the mask of blissful peace...

...becomes a mask of despair and terror. And he dances his last tragic ballet. The audience sits as though turned to stone. He rages through the air like a storm, seeming to hang over the room. "It was like a dance against death." The previous evening he told his wife: "This is not peace. The war in Europe will continue in other, more devious ways. This is only the beginning."

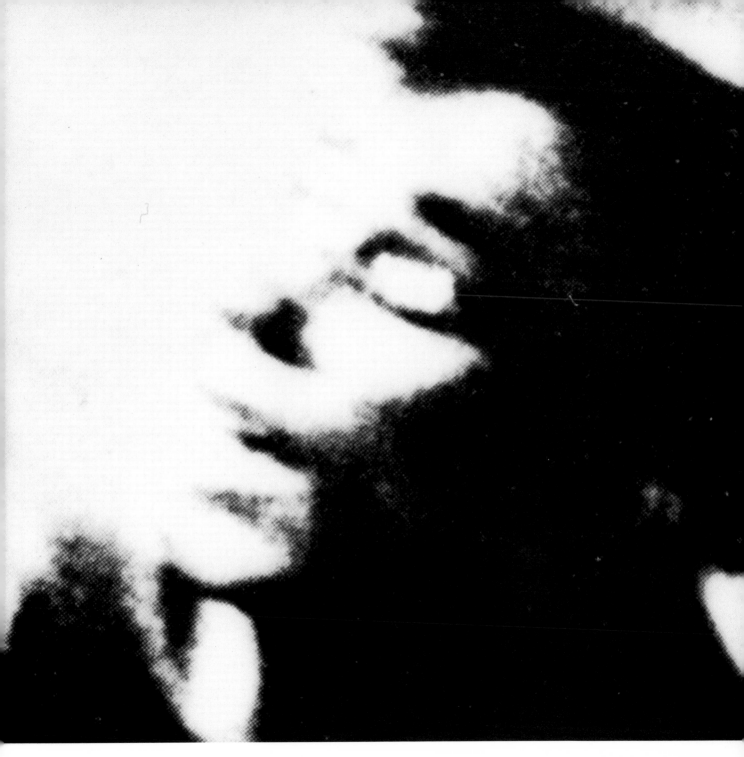

His soaring aerial ballet becomes a dazzling choreographic grotesque. The "Clown of God", as he once termed himself, shows its appalling face. Then, suddenly, it is over. He stops and cries: "Enough!" The following day Romola brings him to Professor Bleuler in Zurich. "Incurable schizophrenia" is the diagnosis. The next day is Nijinsky's thirtieth birthday.

What more can I offer? A great fire, perhaps; a bonfire in honour of paradise and its inventors? But I know only too well that, even if I turn the most bombastic hotel palace into a vast pire, it will be but a paltry offering. A small backstage fire, nothing more. And the props that will go up in flames are no longer in use. The actors who brought them are gone, and their plays no longer performed.

The hour is late. You will be wanting to get home. I hope I have succeeded in amazing you. Please feel free to clear your throats, and speak up if you have any doubts. You will have to excuse me now. As you can see, all hands are needed backstage. Even illusionists.

Where the pictures come from (and what they show):

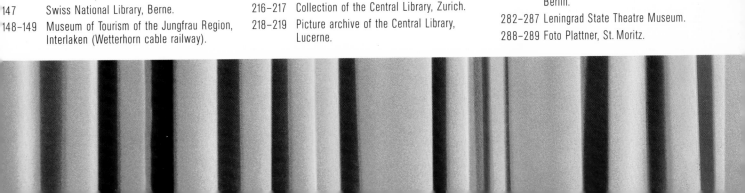

We would like to thank those who have made this spectacle possible:

Beat Curti, Küsnacht.   Eric Franck, Geneva.   And our "Compère" Igor Jozsa, New York.

Our thanks, too, to the following without whose advice, help and enthusiasm the spectacle could not have been put on:

Andrea Badrutt, St. Moritz.   Peter Bally sen., Meilen. Hans Rudolf Bener, Chur.   Rosmarie and Emanuel Berger, Interlaken.   Ellen Berry-Grieder, St. Moritz. David Bon, Regensberg.   Klaus Bon, Hausen bei Brugg. Rudolf Candrian, Zurich.   Paula Carrington, Bath. Elke Claussnitzer, Berlin. The kind ladies of the Russian Library, Zurich.   Fritz Frey, Lucerne.   Peter-Christian Fueter-Corti, Neftenbach.   Bruno Giacometti, Zollikon. Jürgen Glaesemer, Berne.   Liz Gregory, London.   Sarah Hann, London.   Victor Hauser, Lucerne.   Gertrud Hillerbrand, Glattbrugg.   Ralph Hyde, London.   Edgar Kuhn, Berne.   Inneke Maag, Zurich.   Raymond Mander, Sydenham.   Ursula McMullan, London.   Joe Mitchenson, Sydenham.   Beryl M. Häfliger Murray, Bath. Jürg Reinshagen, Lucerne.   Michael Riedler, Lucerne. Agnes Rutz, Zurich.   Rosemarie Seiler, Gletsch/Brig. Anna Shepherd, London.   Liz and Michael Simkin, Olton Solihull.   Christiane Smith, Geneva. David Streiff, Zurich.   Madeleine Keller-Guignard, Zurich.   Trudi Wangler, Lucerne.   Sissi Zöbeli, Zurich.

© Verlagsgesellschaft Beobachter AG, Publishers, Glattbrugg 1983.

Idea, Concept and Manuscript:
Peter Christian Bener and Daniel Schmid.

Design:
Franz Kaufmann, Atelier für Werbung und Design, Zurich.

Text:
Martin Suter, Basel.

Authors' assistant:
Dominik Keller, Zurich.

Translation:
Peter Hill, Dartmouth, GB.

Photos of "Compère":
Hans Gissinger and Daniel Kohlbacher, Zurich.

Retouching:
Nora Fehr, Foto Make ups, Zollikon. Demaris Muhl, Rüfenacht Retouchen, Maur. Schütz + Keller, Retouche-Atelier, Zurich.

Lithographs:
Pesavento AG, Zurich.

Typesetting:
Corso Satz AG, Zurich.

Printed by:
Chemigraphisches Institut AG, Glattbrugg.

Binding:
Maurice Busenhart S.A., Lausanne.
ISBN 3 85569 035 9